SELLING IS EASY

SELLING IS EASY

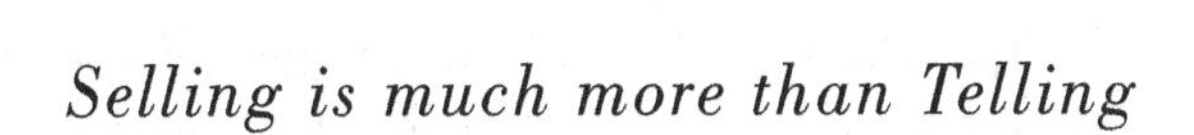

Selling is much more than Telling

Zeaur Rahman

ISBN:	Hardcover	978-1-4828-8268-1
	Softcover	978-1-4828-8267-4
	eBook	978-1-4828-8269-8

Print information available on the last page.

To order additional copies of this book, contact
Toll Free 800 101 2657 (Singapore)
Toll Free 1 800 81 7340 (Malaysia)
orders.singapore@partridgepublishing.com

www.partridgepublishing.com/singapore

I dedicate this book, with deep respect and great love, to my parents, and to all those who have educated me and influenced me in my life's journey up to this point.

ACKNOWLEDGEMENTS

First, I want to thank Almighty God. Second, I thank my parents. In addition, I am thankful to all my teachers, mentors, colleagues, and many writers who have inspired me. I am sharing knowledge which I have internalized during my decade of experience in the field of selling. I have been in sales profession since 2003. I have learned from many people who are much wiser than I, as well as from many other sources. Even though it is not possible to give credit to each person separately, I am deeply indebted to them all. I am also thankful to Liston Thomson, my friend who designed the cover of *Selling Is Easy*.

The people most responsible for helping to make *Selling Is Easy* become a reality are my wife, Dr Shahla Tabassum, and our two wonderful kids, Zishan and Shadan.

If you don't know, learn.
If you already know, apply.
If you know and have applied, improve.

Anonymous

If you want something in your life you've never had, you'll have to do something, you've never done

J D Houston

CONTENTS

INTRODUCTION

Thank you for buying *Selling Is Easy*. It is written to help you achieve your sales target, making you a winner and a great success at your sales job. I trust that this information will allow you to hone your sales skills and become the star sales professional of your company.

In any sales team, the top 20 per cent salespeople bring 80 per cent of the business. This Pareto principle has been proven over and over again since it was formulated in 1895 by Vilfredo Pareto. Your first goal for your career in sales should be to become one of the salespeople in the top 20 per cent of your team. The more knowledge you acquire and the greater skill that you apply, the more competent and valuable you will become.

The first step towards achieving success is to have a clear sense of purpose. Know your goals!

A goal gives you a sense of direction. First you must be very clear in your mind about your goal for your professional life. You want to be a very successful sales professional. You know what you have to do to achieve this, that is by learning selling skills and applying those skills, along with hard work and dedication. You must have an action plan to become a top sales professional. Goals without an action plan are just wishes.

The second step towards becoming a success is to implement your action plan to achieve your goals!

A goal broken down into steps becomes a plan. By writing out the individual steps and then crossing each one off your list as you complete it, you will realize that you are making progress towards your ultimate goal. A plan backed by action makes your dream come true. Just like you cannot learn to swim by reading a book, you cannot be taught to sell in any other way than by practising selling in the field. Do not postpone doing all the things that you need to do in order to achieve your goals. You can achieve your goal to become a star sales professional if you have the discipline to pay the price, if you do what needs to be done, and if you never give up. *Self-discipline is the ability to do what you should do when you should do it, whether you feel like it or not.*

The ability to practise self-discipline is the real reason why some people are more successful and happy than others. Lack of self-discipline is the major cause of failure, frustration, underachievement, and unhappiness in life.

The most important step towards achieving success is to persistently focus to achieve your goal and keep on learning and practising all the skills necessary to achieve your goals.

You should be ambitious with a burning desire to achieve your goal to become a successful sales professional. A positive attitude to learn proven sales skills, clarity about your goal, a burning desire to achieve your goal, and action to transfer your dream into reality is the recipe for your success in sales. *Focus*, if read as an acronym, stands for "finish one course until successful."

Confucius tells us, "The essence of knowledge is, having it, to use it." I hope you enjoy using what you learn from *Selling Is Easy.* As a result, you will be happier and more productive. Yes, selling is easy!

CHAPTER 1

Selling

Sales is one of the world's oldest professions. It is also one of the most exciting, financially rewarding, and challenging professions. A successful salesperson combines attitudes, behaviours, and skills so as to build long-term business relationships with customers that are mutually beneficial for both buyer and seller.

A salesperson sells goods and services to customers. The successfulness of a salesperson is usually measured by the sales he or she is able to make during a given period. Also included is how good he or she is in persuading individuals to make a purchase. The skill of selling is nothing but the transfer of enthusiasm from the seller to the buyer. A good salesperson should have strong belief in the product he or she is selling. Selling is 90 per cent conviction and 10 per cent communication of that conviction. The more you believe in what you sell, the easier it is for you to convince someone else that your product is valuable.

Marketing strategizes the source of revenue, but it is sales that actually bring in the revenue. The purpose for any business is to make money now and in future also, by delivering value to existing and new customers. This is possible only when sales professionals maintain good business relationships based on trust with existing customers, and continue to create new customers.

To become a good sales professional, first you need to learn time-tested proven principles. Next, you must regularly practise these principles on the ground. The first step is to discover what your customers expect and demand, and then to determine what you need to do to meet those expectations and demands. Customers expect you to add value to their business by fully understanding their needs and offering relevant solutions.

An owner of a company invests his or her money to buy inventory. Then he or she hires sales professionals to convert that inventory back to money, but with a profit, and to increase inventory turnover. The good sales professional always tries to increase throughput. *Throughput* is "the rate at which inventory is converted into sales." The good salesperson understands very well that to create a good return, he must sell for a higher margin and maintain a high rate of inventory turnover.

In recent years, selling has increased in complexity, as product and services have become more technical, competition more intense, and buyers more sophisticated. In addition, purchase decisions are now shared by several layers of management and technical experts. The knowledge and skills required to meet the complex and competitive market conditions of today are acquired through intensive training and practice.

In earlier days, demand preceded the supply, and therefore there was no need to put in much effort to sell products. Now, there are more CNC (computer numerical control) machines, so robotics are involved in production. Production is now carried out on a large scale. Also, because of globalization, the size of the market has increased for all producers and manufacturers. One product is produced not by one producer but by several producers in many countries. This results in overproduction and tough competition among the producers.

In any company, the sales department is the only department where cash/revenue is generated. Cash/revenue is the oxygen of any organization, so the sales department, as revenue generator, is the most important department. All other departments serve to support the sales department.

Selling Process

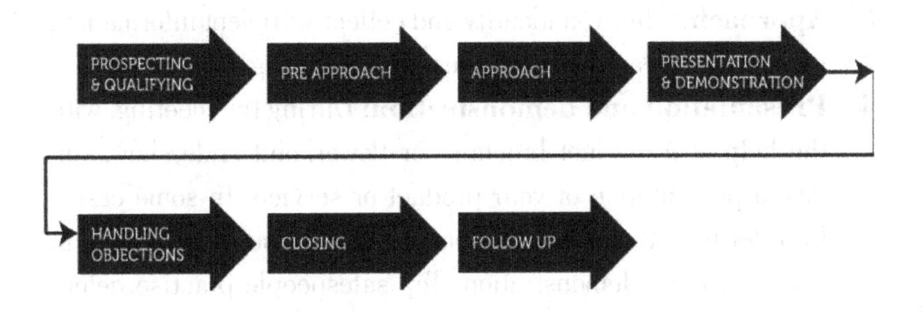

Success does not just happen. It is the result of practising the principles that lead to success.

The steps of the selling process are:

1. prospecting
2. pre-approach
3. approach
4. presentation and demonstration
5. meeting or handling objections
6. closing the sale
7. following up.

1. **Prospecting: This is the first step in the selling process where you identify potential buyers. There are two reasons that a salesperson must constantly be on the lookout for new customers:**

    a. to increase sales
    b. to replace the customers who in time will be lost in time.

2. **Pre-approach**: Once you identify the right segment of customers, next step is to collect information, for example about key decision makers, the location of your prospect, the person's or company's contact details, and the potential customer's ongoing projects.
3. **Approach**: After you identify and collect sufficient information, you then approach your prospect for a meeting.
4. **Presentation and demonstration**: During the meeting, with the help of a product brochure or PowerPoint slide show, you give a presentation of your product or service. In some cases, in order to better persuade your customer, you also arrange to give a product demonstration. Top salespeople practise before giving presentations so that the interpersonal interaction and presentation both seem very convincing and natural. In your presentation, you should provide at least three reasons why the customer should decide to purchase the product from your company. Also, it is very important to make a unique sales proposition and to enumerate the competitive advantages of your products or services.

    Remember the acronym AIDA. The product should be presented or demonstrated in such a way that it

    - gets the customer's *attention*,
    - holds his or her *interest*,

- builds up his or her *desire* for your product or service, and
- ends up in purchase *action.*

5. **Meeting or handling objections**: During your presentation and demonstration, your prospect will ask questions and seek explanations to ease his or her doubts. Your job is to effectively answer these questions in a most convincing and systematic manner. To do this, you need to know your products very well. Also, you have to convince yourself first of the usefulness of your product or service. As has been rightly said, "Selling is 90% conviction and 10% communication of your conviction to your customers."
6. **Closing the sale**: After your presentation and your easing of the prospect's doubt and objection, you should move on to the next stage: asking the prospect to place an order. This is the most important stage. The art of closing the sale needs to be developed by each sales professional.
7. **Following up**: It is important for you as a salesperson to make sure a PDI (pre-delivery inspection) is done, the product is delivered on time, and payment is received. Good follow-up builds goodwill and encourages repeat purchases.

Importance of Follow-up in Sales

One of the reasons salespeople fail is that they do not follow up with customers in a timely manner. *Too much or too little follow-up is dangerous.* Timely follow-up builds credibility and trust with customers. Good follow-up keeps the customer informed. As a result, customers value you and see you as being more reliable than those salespeople working for businesses competing with yours. Following up shows your caring attitude and makes the customer feel important and happy. If you don't want to lose customers to your competition, then ensure timely follow-up with your clients. Customers prefer not to work with those salespeople whom they find to be unreliable.

There are some interesting sales statistics regarding follow-up and deal closing. These are:

- Forty-eight per cent of salespeople never follow up with a prospect.
- Twenty-five per cent of salespeople make a second contact with the prospect and then stop.
- Twelve per cent of salespeople only make three contacts and then stop.
- Only fifteen per cent of salespeople make more than three contacts with a prospect.

Customers do business with those they know, like, and trust. This is supported by the following information:

- Two per cent of sales are made on the first contact.
- Three per cent of sales are made on the second contact.
- Five per cent of sales are made on the third contact.
- Ten per cent of sales are made on the fourth contact.
- Eighty per cent of sales are made on the fifth to twelfth contact.

You should use the right combination of direct emails, telephonic calls, and personal visits to make your follow-ups more effective. First you should make a direct visit to the prospect's place of business. This should be followed by timely emails, telephone calls, and follow-up visits. During the direct visit, you should use both verbal and non-verbal communication skills to influence your potential customers and develop a relation based on respect and trust.

Remember, professional selling is problem solving and helping customers after you come to understand their need. Because the customer has a need, you have a job to do. Because the customer has a choice, you must be the better choice. Because of the customer, your business exists! The management consultant Peter Drucker said, "There is only one purpose of business: to create customer."[1]

Customers prefer salespersons whom they know, like, and trust. Trustworthiness and hard work coupled with sales skills can transform an ordinary salesperson into very successful sales professional. The good sales professional first tries to understand the need of the customer. Only then does she mention the best product which will be of great value to the customer and profit his or her company.

The good sales professional continuously develops the following soft skills, which are discussed in details in the chapters indicated:

- understanding selling and the selling process (discussed in Chapter 1)
- having a positive mental attitude (discussed in Chapter 2)
- being motivated and practising self-discipline (discussed in Chapter 3)
- having ambition and desire (discussed in Chapter 4)
- developing a pleasing personality and trustworthiness (discussed in Chapter 5)

---

[1] Peter Drucker, *The Practice of Management* (New York: Harper & Row, 1954), 38–39.

- being goal oriented and having a clear sales target (discussed in Chapter 6)
- working hard and being persistent in one's efforts (discussed in Chapter 7)
- learning the art of communicating with customers (discussed in Chapter 8)
- learning the art of dealing with customers (discussed in Chapter 9)
- learning about sales skills and competencies (discussed in Chapters 11, 12, and 13)
- learning the art of handling objections (discussed in Chapter 12)
- learning the art of closing the sale (discussed in Chapter 13)
- learning proven sales strategies (discussed in Chapter 14)
- learning marketing concepts (discussed in Chapter 15)
- learning the concepts of segmentation, targeting, and positioning (discussed in Chapter 16)
- understanding what customers want (discussed in Chapter 17)
- learning time management (discussed in Chapter 18)
- avoiding mistakes and learning from the experience of others (discussed in Chapter 19)
- learning how to employ ethics in selling (discussed in Chapter 20).

As previously mentioned, as a sales professional you should first understand the need of customer. Then you should suggest the product or service which will meet that need. Just as writing a prescription before diagnosing a patient shows negligence and unprofessional conduct on the doctor's part, trying to sell without understanding the need of customer is the surest way for a salesperson to fail. Sales and marketing entrepreneur Tony Alessandra said, "In selling as well as in medicine prescription before diagnosis is malpractice."

Robert Louis Stevenson said something I agree with: "I find it useful to remember, everyone lives by selling something." Our selling ability determines the success or failure of any transaction we engage in. Everyone is selling something to someone directly or indirectly.

- Lawyers argue their client's case in court.
- Politicians make speeches to their voters in rallies.
- Candidates seek a job during interviews.
- Interviewers seek to recruit new employees.
- Parents deal with their kids at home.
- Teachers/professors deal with students at schools/colleges.

The salespeople control the experience, as they are the ones who directly contact the customers. They should provide a great experience for their customers by building a relationship based on trust and practising empathy. Professional salesperson always:

- build relationships with customers based on trust
- practise empathy
- educate customers
- understand customer psychology and have insight into consumers.

Selling is an inner game. Eighty per cent of selling is the result of self-esteem, self-image, and mental conditioning. Only twenty per cent consists of sales skills. The way you think and feel about yourself gets communicated to others. If you feel good about yourself, your product, and your company, then this gets communicated non-verbally to the prospect.

Management guru David Maister famously said, "Customer don't care how much you know until they know how much you care." There is an old saying, "If you see John Jones with John Jones's eyes, then you can sell John Jones what John Jones buys." If you care about your potential customers and can understand their perspective, selling then becomes easy!

"I find it useful to remember, everyone lives by selling something"

Robert Louis Stennson

In selling as in medicine prescription before diagnosis is malpractice

Tonv Allasandra

CHAPTER 2

Positive Mental Attitude

> None can destroy Iron but its own rust can! Likewise, none can destroy a person but his own mindset can.
> Ratan Tata

> The pessimist sees difficulty in every opportunity. The optimist sees the opportunity in every difficulty.
> Winston Churchill

Iron reacting with oxygen rusts when moisture or water is present. We paint iron to prevent it from rusting. In a similar process, our mindset is affected when we come into contact with evil and negativity. To prevent a negative mindset, you must guard your mind against any negative thoughts. Continually remove negative thoughts from your mind as a gardener regularly removes weeds from his garden. Your mind is your garden. Your thoughts are seeds. You can grow flowers or you can grow weeds; the choice is yours. The moment a negative thought enters your mind, replace it with a positive thought. At any one moment, you can have only one thought. Make it a habit to avoid negative thoughts and to think positively. Don't be the prisoner of the past; be the architect of the future. You need to train your brain to think about the future and to refrain from thinking about negative past events.

Sales depends more upon the attitude of the sales professional than upon that of the prospect. Let me tell you a story often told by sales managers. Two salesmen went to different parts of Africa to sell shoes. They both encountered many villagers without shoes. One of the salesmen immediately sent a message back to his manager saying, "There is no market here. Nobody wears shoes. I am returning home."

The other salesman sent a message saying, "Get ready for big sales. There is a huge market here. Nobody wears shoes. We have the opportunity to make everyone want to wear them. Gear up production."

You can't change the world, but you can change how you perceive it and how you react to it. The good sales professional always thinks positive and remains an optimist. She always sees half a glass of water as half-full, not half-empty. Mind management is the essence of life management. See the glass as half-full, and then fill it the rest of the way. Your attitude towards your job can determine whether your days are filled with excitement and the sense of fulfilment that comes from top performance or with frustration, boredom, and fatigue.

Following is a very interesting and meaningful message I want to share with you:

If A, B, C, D, E, F, G, H, I, J, K, L, M, N, O, P, Q, R, S, T, U, V, W, X, Y, and Z are respectively equal to 1, 2, 3, 4, 5, 6, 7, 8, 9, 10, 11, 12, 13, 14, 15, 16, 17, 18, 19, 20, 21, 22, 23, 24, 25, and 26, in percentage form, then the following things are true:

L+U+C+K	= 12+21+3+11	= 47%
K+N+O+W+L+E+D+G+E	= 11+14+15+23+12+5+4+7+5	= 96%
L+E+A+D+E+R+S+H+I+P	= 12+5+1+4+5+18+19+8+9+16	= 97%
H+A+R+D + W+O+R+K	= 8+1+18+4 + 23+15+18+11	= 98%

Every problem has a solution, only if we change our attitude.

A+T+T+I+T+U+D+E =1+20+20+9+20+21+4+5 = 100%

It is therefore our attitude towards life and work that makes our life 100 per cent successful.

Whatever you expect with confidence becomes a self-fulfilling prophecy. Your expectations exert an undue influence on the people around you. Your expectations determine your attitude, and your attitude determines how you treat other people. The rule with regard to expectations is always to expect the best. Expect that people will like you. Look forward to people being attracted to your product or service. Incorporate an attitude of positive expectancy into your sales activities and people will treat you well, as you expected. You will also make more sales.

When you make the mistake of negatively prejudging a prospect, you lose your enthusiasm. Your attitude will reveal to the prospect that you don't really believe in the product/service or the prospect's ability to buy what you are selling. The prospect will discern this from your attitude and will not buy from you.

Whatever your mind can conceive and believe, you can achieve. The only limitation is the limitation in your mind. Success comes to those who become success-conscious. Failure comes to those who allow themselves to become failure-conscious. You have the power to control your thoughts. If you think you can, then you will; if you think you can't, then you won't.

Mental conditioning is done through a process of autosuggestion and visualization. This is a process used by some of the top sports professionals and athletes in the world. Visualization is a process of forming a mental picture. A picture of success translates into success in life. Autosuggestions are positive statements regarding the kind of person you want to be or the things you want to do. Regularly visualize yourself as a top sales professional. Also do self-talk, repeating, "Every day I am becoming a better sales professional than I was yesterday."

During religious gatherings, I've noticed the imam during sermons asking the faithful to visualize heaven and hell and then explaining that if you follow the right path, you will go to heaven, and if you follow the wrong path, it will lead you to hell. During the Islamic prayers called namaz or salah, at every step everyone says, "Allahu Akbar," which literally means "Allah is greatest." Here, by using the principle of autosuggestion, we are developing faith in God.

You can't live a positive life with a negative mind. Athlete and entrepreneur Lewis Howes said, "Life is better if you develop an attitude of gratitude." This means that you make it habit to express thankfulness and appreciation for all things in your life, big and small alike, on a regular basis. Easy steps to develop positive mental attitude are as follows:

1. Acknowledge yourself for what you have done and accomplished. Never compare yourself with others. Instead, compete with yourself.
2. Start a gratitude journal. Learn to express gratitude in this journal by noting the things that you are grateful for.
3. Acknowledge other people and thank them for each thing they do for you. Oftentimes people wait their whole lives to be acknowledged. Practise saying thank you and being sincerely appreciative.
4. Always expect the best. Start every morning by saying, "I believe something wonderful is going to happen to me today." Repeat it over and over.

Ability is how to do something. Motivation is why we do something. Attitude determines how well we do.

"If you can see a positive side to everything, you'll be able to live a much richer life than others"

Celestine Chua

See the glass half full and fill it the rest of the Way

Unknown

CHAPTER 3

Motivation and Self-Discipline

> People often say Motivation doesn't last, well ... neither does bathing, that's why we recommend it daily.
>
> Zig Ziglar

> The man who has confidence in himself gains the confidence of others.
>
> Hasidic proverb

Motivation sits behind discipline. It is hard to be disciplined when you have no motivation. The more difficult something becomes, the more we don't like doing it, and therefore the more motivation we need to be disciplined. Motivation is like a fire. Unless we keep adding fuel, it dies out. Fuel to a good sales professional is the positive thoughts fed to your mind on a daily basis, combined with clarity of your goals or sales target.

In the year 2009 I was working in sales in the United Arab Emirates. Because there was a recession, almost all of the new construction had slowed down and lot of ongoing projects were stopped. Every morning it was very tough for me to decide whom I would call and which customer I would meet, as I was dealing in a product related to the construction industry badly hit by recession. Lots of small- and medium-sized companies were closing, almost on a daily basis. During my meetings with customers, we hardly discussed the business. Even the purchase managers and workshop managers were unsure about their job security. Those days were very frustrating, especially for sales professionals. Every company was downsizing and reducing their number of employees. My biggest challenge was to keep myself motivated. I purchased some audiobooks related to sales and motivation. I found these things to be very useful in keeping me motivated. Also, I enrolled myself in an evening MBA course at S. P. Jain Centre of Management, Dubai. Because I developed the habit of listening to audiobooks during my travelling, and because I was attending evening classes, I became more skilled in my day job, which helped me to retain my job, as I became more productive than before.

My company introduced some new products which were of good value for the money. This strategy worked. What we did is best described by something Winston Churchill said: "The optimist sees the opportunity in every difficulty."

Some salespeople, as soon as achieve their monthly sales target, stop working. This is because they only want to keep their job; they are not internally motivated to exceed expectations. To a good sales professional, every sale is exciting. It gives them satisfaction.

If you want to be physically fit and healthy, then you have to avoid junk foods, take proper rest, and exercise regularly. Similarly, if you want to be mentally fit, then you must avoid all forms of negative influence and regularly feed your mind with the right kinds of books, podcasts, and seminars, and keep yourself in the company of positive and successful people. You must make every effort to ensure that the mental influences around you are as positive as possible. If you read unconstructive material in books, magazines, or newspapers, or watch violent programmes on television or the Internet, then your mind becomes filled with mental garbage that can demotivate you and make you more easily discouraged. The human mind is very much like computer. The choice is yours regarding which kind of information you feed to your mind. Consider the acronym GIGO, which means "goods in and goods out" or "garbage in and garbage out." The choice is yours!

You must choose your friends and associates with care. As Zig Ziglar says, "You cannot fly with the eagles if you continue to scratch with the turkeys." Be around positive people. Socialize with folks who are positive and who have goals for themselves and their work. Only spend time with people who have virtues that you admire and want to emulate. Meanwhile, get away from negative people. Avoid those who complain and criticize much of the time. Especially avoid joining in when people start complaining about their work or about other successful people.

The easy steps to keep you motivated are:

- Determine your goals.
- Maintain a positive attitude.
- Put personal problems aside when you are at work.
- Upgrade your knowledge and skills.
- Be passionate. Love your job.
- Decrease or eliminate energy drains. Avoid negative thinking. Avoid people who always criticize and backbite.
- Practise self-talk. Use autosuggestions, positive statements about the kind of person you want to be.
- Confront challenges and fears. Do the thing you fear.
- Meditate, as knowing yourself is the beginning of all wisdom.
- Acknowledge and reward success.

Self-Discipline

> You were born to win, but to be a winner; you must plan to win, prepare to win and expect to win.
>
> Zig Ziglar

> Talent without discipline is like an octopus on roller skates. There's plenty of movement, but you never know if it's going to be forward, backwards, or sideways.
>
> H. Jackson Brown Jr.

As previously mentioned, you can achieve almost any goal you set for yourself if you have the discipline to pay the price, to do what you need to do, and to never give up. Self-discipline is the ability to do what you should do when you should do it, whether you feel like it or not. There is direct relationship between self-discipline and self-esteem. Self-discipline is the key to self-esteem and self-respect.

Just as self-discipline is the key to success, the lack of self-discipline is the major cause of failure, frustration, underachievement, and unhappiness in life. The absence of self-discipline leads us to make excuses and sell ourselves short. Self-discipline is the bridge between goals and accomplishments. It is the distance between your dream and reality which you have to cover if you want to accomplish your goals.

H. L. Hunt, owner of more than two hundred companies and at one time the richest man in the world, was once asked for his "secret of success." He replied, "I have started and built hundreds of companies. In fifty years of experience, I have found that there are only two things necessary for success: decide exactly what you want (most people never do this), and determine the price that you are going to pay to get what you want and then resolve to pay that price."

The difference between *who you are* and *who you want to be* is *what you do*. No one can motivate you until you motivate yourself. As Zig Ziglar said, "You were born to win, but to be a winner; you must plan to win, prepare to win and expect to win."

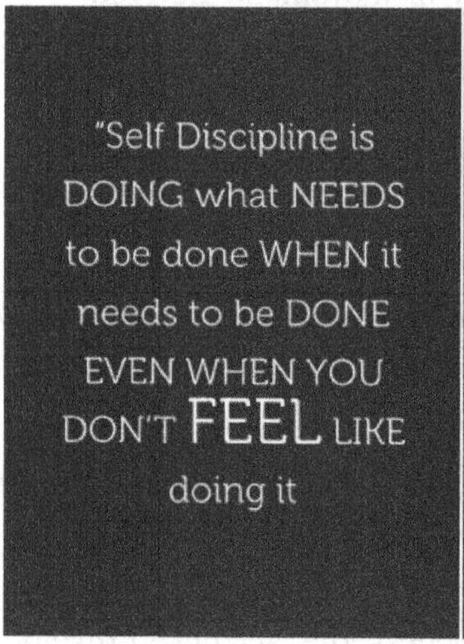

"Self Discipline is DOING what NEEDS to be done WHEN it needs to be DONE EVEN WHEN YOU DON'T FEEL LIKE doing it

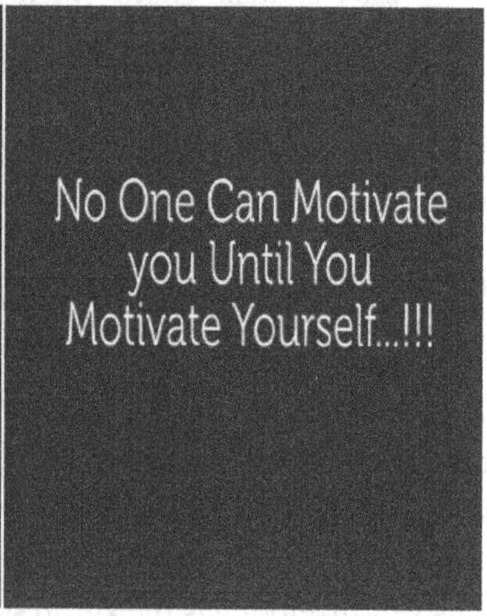

No One Can Motivate you Until You Motivate Yourself...!!!

CHAPTER 4

Ambition and Desire

> Intelligence without ambition is a bird without wings.
>
> Salvador Dali

> Whatever the mind of man can conceive and believe, it can achieve. When thoughts are mixed with definiteness of purpose and burning desire, it can be translated into riches.
>
> Napoleon Hill

Every accomplishment starts with the decision to try. Ambition is a strong desire to meet a particular objective, especially the drive to succeed or to gain fame, power, wealth, etc. Ambition is enthusiasm with purpose. Ambition and desire are the foundation qualities of all great achievements. Selling has often been defined as a transfer of enthusiasm. Top salespeople have above-average ambition and desire to sell. Top salespeople have a burning commitment and an intense desire to be successful. They will not let anything stop them. To put it another way, they are "hungry." Average salespeople think in terms of making just enough money to pay their bills. Once they achieve their minimum monthly sales target, they stop putting their efforts towards achieving sales. They don't believe in putting in the extra effort that is essential for great success. They forget that at

99°C, hot water remains hot water, but at 100°C hot water turns to steam. An additional degree transforms hot water into steam, which concept is useful and has many applications.

Ambition is both very important in life and essential for great success. It is the chief motivator that propels us to achieve great things. It is the driving force which makes us do things to get better in life. Surround yourself with people who have dreams, desire, and ambition. They will help you push for and realize your own dreams.

Steps to achieve success are as follows:

1. Firmly believe in yourself. Always picture yourself as successful. Develop a positive mental attitude.
2. Have clear goals when it comes to what you want to achieve in your life and career.
3. When you begin to deviate from these goals, take immediate corrective action.
4. Have a burning desire to achieve your goals.

A long time ago, a great warrior had to pit his army against a powerful foe, whose men outnumbered his own. He loaded his soldiers into boats, and they sailed to the enemy's country. After they reached their destination, he ordered his soldiers to burn the boats. Then he addressed his men before battle, saying, "The boats have been burnt. We cannot leave these shores alive unless we win. We now have no choice. Either we win or we perish!" His army fought with a burning desire to win. They won the battle!

Brad Burden said that winners must have two things:

1. definite goals and
2. a burning desire to achieve them.

Ambition is the path to success, and persistence is the vehicle you arrive in. Persistence is the ability to bounce back after every rejection. Lack of persistence can cause you to lose the deal. When you do this, you actually end up selling for your competitors. Once when Winston Churchill visited a school, the students asked him the secret of his success. After one of his famous pauses, he replied with just seven words: "Never give up. Never, ever give up." Once you have clear goals and a burning desire to achieve those goals, you must be persistently focused with a "never give up attitude" until you achieve your goal. Again, *focus* as an acronym means "finish one course until successful."

"AMBITION
is the path to success.
PERSISTENCE
is the vehicle you arrive in

CHAPTER 5

Pleasing Personality and Trustworthiness

> A pleasant personality helps you win friends and influence people. Add character to that formula and keep those friends and maintain influence.
>
> Zig Ziglar

> If people like you they will listen to you but if they trust you they will do business with you.
>
> Zig Ziglar

Pleasing Personality

In sales, your pleasing personality and trustworthiness are more important than the product or service that you are selling. Top salespeople take proper care of their physical body as well as their mind, keeping both fit. They eat a healthy diet and regularly do exercise to keep themselves physically fit and active. They regularly read books and listen to audio programs related to sales, and regularly practise those skills that make them mentally fit for the sales job. They have a high level of self-confidence and self-esteem. Without self-confidence, it is almost impossible to be successful in selling. The more you like yourself, the more you like others. When you like your customers, then customers will like you and listen to you. First impressions are crucial, as people form opinions about one another within the first three to five seconds of meeting, even before a person says anything. In order to create a favourable first impression, it is important that you do the following things:

- Appear well groomed, neat, and clean.
- Dress formally for business appointments. I personally prefer a plain light-coloured long-sleeve dress shirt, dark-coloured trousers, a matching tie, and shined black shoes.
- Greet others with a pleasant smile and a firm handshake. (A firm handshake does not mean crushing the prospect's hand. Instead, your handshake should show warmth.)
- Wear pleasant-smelling perfume or aftershave.

You will never get second chance to create a first impression.

To create a positive impact, you need to have a pleasing personality. A pleasing personality is a composite of overall behaviour, appearance, verbal and non-verbal communication, dress, grooming, etiquette, and manners. Positive and polite words always lead to pleasantness. The composite personality reflects in our people skills, which is the starting point of rapport building. A sales professional is an ambassador for both her product and the company. Burt Lancaster said, "Sell yourself first if you want to sell anything to your customer." To create a good impression, you have to build rapport, gain confidence, and build trust with the prospect. Remember that the first thing you have to sell is yourself. In fact, your pleasing personality plays a very important role in your sales success. A successful salesperson develops good relationships with his colleagues, immediate boss, and customers that are based on trust and respect. He genuinely believes in team spirit. He knows that the word *team*, read as an acronym, stands for "Together everyone achieves more."

The successful sales professional believes in teamwork. She develops professional work relationships with colleagues in the marketing department, logistics department, and purchasing department, and with her sales colleagues, the office staff, supervisors, and managers. Getting along with people is a must for any sales professional. With teamwork and collaboration, wonderful things can be achieved. As Dalal Haldeman, senior vice president for marketing and communications for Johns Hopkins Medicine, said, "Individual talents get magnified many times over through the collective lens of an effective team." Since sales professionals are the eyes and ears for their company, as they are the ones who meet directly with customers, they must communicate effectively to the marketing department any noticeable change in the marketplace. Lack of synergy between the sales department and the marketing department is one of the reasons for failure of the sales professional. Sometimes during the sales visit, the prospect asked about the products which other sales professionals of another department of his company are handling. The sales professional then shares this information with his colleagues. This way, not only does she increase sales for her company, but also she demonstrates her pleasing personality to her customer because of her "team player" attitude. In return she also gets leads for selling products or services to another department. This type of salesperson understands very well that *team*, read as an acronym, means "Together everyone achieves more."

Trustworthiness

Trust takes years to build, seconds to break, and forever to repair. Successful sales professionals develop themselves as responsible, honest, trustworthy, and hard-working people. Customers trust them. They always give the right suggestions to customers and become their customers' reliable single point of contact.

There is no substitute for honesty in selling. American radio personality Earl Nightingale once said, "If honesty did not exist, it would have to be invented as the surest way of getting rich." Top salespeople are honest with themselves and with their customers.

One research study that including interviewing several customers to find out why they bought from one salesperson or company and not from other, even though the products were similar, arrived at a simple conclusion: customers bought from one salesperson instead of the others because they trusted that person more. The top sales professional fulfils all his promises and remains committed to keeping his customers satisfied. Top sales professionals have a high level of empathy, that is they really care about their customers. The desire to achieve combined with genuinely caring about the well-being of your customers are the twin keys to top sales performance. Empathy is the most important of all character traits for building and maintaining high-quality relationships with other people. A salesperson with empathy makes every effort to get inside the mind and heart of the customer and to understand his situation and needs. Remember the saying mentioned in Chapter 1: "If you can see John Jones through John Jones's eyes, then you can sell John Jones what John Jones buys."

Empathy requires the development of a long-term perspective. Average salespeople think primarily in terms of making a sale right now, with little concern for long-term relationships or future sales. Top salespeople, on the other hand, think about the future sales potential to this customer while still talking to her about the first sale. Salespeople who think like this know that profit in business comes from repeat customers. They know the value of having lifetime customers. As a result, they are far more empathetic in the short term than average salespeople.

A balance between ambition and empathy seems to be the ideal combination for long-term sales success. If a salesperson is too ambitious, she will try to force the sale. Customers will sense this. On the other hand, if a salesperson is too empathetic, she will not push for the sale. Balance is essential.

Trust = (credibility × intimacy) / risk

The trust formula shows that your credibility and your relationship with the customer are directly proportional to trust. But trust is inversely proportional to the level of risk involved in a customer's making a purchase decision. To be successful, you must learn to manage risk by asking yourself, *What can I do to make any commitments less risky for the customer?* There is a famous marketing adage: "Nobody ever got fired for buying IBM." The risk is much lower in buying from a well-known company with a worldwide reputation than from a less-established company.

If you have dissatisfied customers, then you cannot continue to make a profit. Buyer perception needs to be corrected at right time. If you have a dissatisfied customer, then your first priority is to find out the reason for the customer's unhappiness so you can sort out the problem as soon as possible. Zig Ziglar said, "If people like you, they will listen to you. But if they trust you, they will do business with you."

A plesing personality helps win friends and influence people. Add character to that formula, and keep those friends and maintain that influence.

Zig Ziglar

If People Like You They Will Listen To You, But If They Trust You, They'll Do Business With You.

Zig Ziglar

CHAPTER 6

Goal Setting

> Dreams are free. Goals have a cost. While you can daydream for free, goals don't come without a price. Time, Effort, Sacrifice and Sweat. How will you pay for your goals?
>
> Usain Bolt

> People are not lazy. They simply have impotent goals i.e. Goals that do not inspire them.
>
> Anthony Robbins

Goal setting starts with your dream. This is followed by how you want to achieve your dream, that is your action plan, which addresses both your dream and your strategy to achieve your goal. A dream written down with a projected date of completion becomes a goal. A goal broken down into steps becomes a plan. A plan backed by action makes your dream come true. People with goals succeed because they know where they are going. How can you reach a destination that you have not defined? A proposed destination determines the direction of your travel. A goal gives you a sense of direction and helps you remain focused on your goal. A goal without a plan is just a wish. Setting a goal is the first step of turning an invisible hope into a visible reality.

Goal achievement requires commitment. You must have an "I must do this" attitude, along with a sense of urgency, to achieve your goal. Goals should be "smart":

- **s**pecific,
- **m**easurable,
- **a**ttainable,
- **r**elevant, and
- **t**ime bound.

Set specific goals: Your goal must be specific.

Set measurable goals: Your goal must be measurable.

Set attainable goals: Your goal should be achievable.

Set relevant goals: Your goal should be important and in line with your other life and career goals.

Set time-bound goals: Your goal must have a deadline.

Your goal must be written on paper, along with all the steps required to achieve the goal. By writing your goal on paper, you make it real and tangible. I prefer to tape the paper on which I've written my goal to my cupboard, as that way I see it every morning as a reminder. By making an action plan, you decide how to achieve your goal in steps.

Goal setting is an ongoing activity. Tell your friends and spouse about your goal, and then walk your talk. Review your goal regularly. If the plan doesn't work, then change the plan – but never the goal. As Zig Ziglar said, "When obstacles arise, you change your direction to reach your goal, you do not change your decision to get there."

How to Achieve Your Sales Target

Divide your yearly sales target into gradations, from largest to smallest: annually, quarterly, monthly, weekly, and daily.

Write down your goals and read them daily. Write down your monthly and daily goals on a sheet of paper you keep in your office just to make sure you keep meeting your daily goals. If you meet your daily goals, you will automatically meet your weekly, monthly, and yearly goals, but if you are behind on your daily goals, it disturbs the timing of the other goals as well. When this happens, you have to take corrective action to achieve your goal.

Many times, salespeople fail because the sales targets have been made unilaterally and without any consideration of resources. A good sales professional should get involved and ask the company to jointly identify the goals and provide the necessary resources to achieve the desired results.

There are some interesting statistics regarding goal setting. It was found that people who wrote down their goals were 42 per cent more likely to achieve them than the ones who didn't. Telling a friend or spouse about your goals increases this rate to 78 per cent.

The tragedy of life doesn't lie in not reaching your goal. The tragedy lies in having no goals to reach. As Oliver Wendell Holmes said, "The greatest thing in this world is not so much where we are, but in which direction we are moving."

Success starts with a dream. Add faith and it becomes a belief. Add action and it becomes a part of life. Add perseverance and it becomes a goal in sight. Add patience and time and it ends with a dream come true.

IF THE PLAN DOEST NOT WORK
CHANGE THE PLAN
BUT NEVER THE GOAL

"To succeed in your mission, you must have single-minded devotion to your goal."

A. P. J. Abdul Kalam

CHAPTER 7

Hard Work and Persistence

> Hard work beats talent when talent doesn't work hard.
>
> Tim Notke

> Patience, persistence and perspiration make an unbeatable combination for success.
>
> Napoleon Hill

The dictionary is the only place where success comes before work. There is no elevator to success; you have to take the stairs. As is said in the Bible, "Whatever a man soweth, that shall he also reap" (Galatians 6:7 King James Version). So plant your seeds. Work hard, as there is no substitute for hard work. As Thomas Edison said, "Success is 95% perspiration and 5% inspiration."

Successful people in any field have one thing common: they work harder than average people. Thomas Stanley, in his book *The Millionaire Next Door*, writes that 85 per cent of the self-made millionaires he interviewed attribute their success to hard work. Average people may want to work hard, but they see it happening sometime in the future, as they lack self-discipline. "The harder I work, the luckier I get." That old line remains true. Work hard to achieve professional excellence. Life helps those who help themselves. For success, we need both will and skill. There are many skilful people who are incompetent because they lack the will. Competence is having the will and the skill to create a positive outcome.

Successful salespeople work much harder than average salespeople. They arrive to work a little earlier and stay a little later. They make sure that they gather all the information required for every stage of the sales process. They gather all the information they can pertaining to the customer's industry and the marketplace. They regularly check customers' websites to get the latest updates on their business before approaching customers face-to-face. They spend the time required to understand the customer's product specification, the unique sales proposition of their product, and the product's competitive advantage. They regularly monitor competitors' activities and customer perception of the competitors' products. They also rehearse their presentation repeatedly and practise asking relevant questions, responding objections, and closing techniques. Customers place more trust in those salespeople who know more about their products, the marketplace, and the customer's industry.

The average salesperson wastes a full 50 per cent of his working time. According to the aforementioned research, he comes in to the office a little later, works a little slower, and leaves a little earlier. He spends most of his workday engaging in idle chit-chat with co-workers, attending to personal business, reading the newspaper, drinking tea, and surfing the Internet.

There is no substitute for persistence. One of the major reasons people failure in sales is their lack of persistence. Many salespeople give up too soon and find it very difficult to handle rejection. The average salesperson doesn't follow up with prospects, gives up easily, and is unable to close the sale.

In one survey seeking to discover why some people are successful and others are failures, the following was found:

- Successful people reach a decision promptly, and if required to change their mind, change their mind very slowly.
- Failures fail to reach a decision, reach decisions very slowly, and change their mind frequently and quickly.

Persistence is very important for success in any field. One of the most common causes of failure is the habit of quitting when one suffers temporary defeat. There is famous old story about a gold prospector in Africa. He claimed land and started exploring it with pick and shovel. After weeks of hard labour of his men, gold was discovered. The man needed machinery to bring the ore to the surface. He took out loans and purchased the required equipment. Initially he brought up the ore and sent it to a smelter. He found that the gold was of good quality, and was happy to project that few more carloads of that ore would clear all his debt. Then something happened – the vein of gold ore disappeared. His men drilled on desperately, trying to pick up the vein again, but to no avail. Finally the prospector decided to quit. He sold the machinery to a junkman. The junkman was smart and called a mining engineer. The engineer, after making some calculations, advised that the vein would be found just three feet from where the men had stopped drilling. That junkman earned millions of dollar from the mine. The gold prospector recouped his losses many times over in his new business of selling insurance, just by developing one habit of stickability, which he learned after quitting the gold mining business. Whenever his customer said no when he asked them to buy insurance, he, remembering that he had lost a huge fortune in his earlier business because he had stopped three feet from gold, persisted in persuading the person to buy an insurance policy from him.

Research shows that 80 per cent of all sales are made after the fifth call and that 80 per cent of salespeople quit before the fifth call. This latter practice is called selling for your competitors. The 80 per cent who quit have prepared the ground and made the buyers ready to purchase. They have done the difficult work, but when the time came to close the sale, they ran out of steam and quit. Now when the competitor calls and sees the client ready to purchase, they come in and close the sale. When you quit, you have actually made the sale for your competitors. Selling is a rejection business. You get more noes than yesses. For the good sales professional, rejection is an opportunity to bounce back. For successful salespeople, *no* is an acronym meaning "next opportunity."

Thomas Edison said, "Many of life's failures are people who did not realize how close they were to success when they gave up."

The Dictionary is the Only Place Where Success Comes Before Work

---

Arthur Brisbane

"Many of life's failures are people who did not realize how close they were to success when they gave up."

Thomas Edision

CHAPTER 8

Art of Communicating with Customers

> When you talk, you are only repeating what you already know. But if you listen, you may learn something new.
>
> Dalai Lama

> Most people think "Selling" is the same as "Talking" but the most effective sales people know that "Listening" is the most important part of their job.
>
> Roy Bartell

Research shows that the first few seconds you spent with a client influences his or her satisfaction more than the minutes of service that follow. Remember the adage "Your first impression is your last impression." Your body language, your facial expression, and the way you greet people all play a very important role in making your first impression. You never get a second chance to make a good first impression. The fact is that when you first meet a person, she makes an opinion about you in approximately four seconds, and her opinion is finalized largely within thirty seconds of the initial contact.

One study shows that 60 per cent of our communication is non-verbal, which includes facial expressions, body language, and tone of voice. The moment you meet a new person, the primitive area of his or her brain puts you into one of four categories based on your body language and facial expression:

1. friend
2. enemy or predator
3. potential sex partner
4. indifferent.

As per behavioural psychologists, when you meet any new person, he or she will not pay attention to you unless you get yourself into the category of friend. You should signal the primitive brain of your customers so as to trigger them to put you in the friend category.

Art of Listening

In selling, it is hard to resist talking. Sometimes you appear too eager to sell and too inclined not to listen. But customers will listen to you only after you show that you will listen to them. Good sales professionals ask relevant questions, listen carefully to identify the needs of the customer, and provide the right solutions. Always wait a few seconds before answering a customer's question. Listen and pause before you speak. By the simple act of listening, you make your client feel important. Most people's idea of listening is waiting until the other person has finished speaking. And the sad fact is that while someone else is talking, most of us are rehearsing our replies in our mind. Listen twice as much as you speak. Become a world-class listener.

The human body is amazing. We have been given two eyes, two ears, and one mouth. These features should be used in that proportion.

Learn to listen and observe twice as much as you talk. If you do this, then you will surely succeed in sales.

To understand a customer's need, you need to develop art of listening and ask relevant questions. Marketing guru Theodore Levitt famously said, "People don't want to buy a quarter inch drill. They want a quarter inch hole." Customers' real needs are sometimes hidden behind an apparent solution. The more questions you ask of your customer, the more success you will enjoy. The salesperson who understands his customers' need better is more successful than others.

As businessman Stephen Covey said, "Seek first to understand, then to be understood." The more time you invest in understanding your customer's need, the greater chance you have of making the sale in the end. Trying to sell your product or service without understanding the customer's need is the surest way to fail.

Body Language

The right body language changes not only the way other people view you but also the way you feel about yourself. If you want to be influential, then you should learn to use 100 per cent of your communication ability, verbal as well as non-verbal.

You should avoid low-power postures. In low-power positions, you generally

- contract your body,
- keep your head down, and
- hunch your shoulders.

When you do these things, you both look and feel less confident.

In the ideal power position, you not only look confident but also feel confident. In this position you generally

- expand your body, loosening your arms,
- keep your shoulders down,
- keep your head up.

Facial Expression

Imagine that your brain is a projector and your face is a screen, and then consider that what you think reflects on your face. Even nearly undetectable facial expressions lasting half a second or less give away how you feel. Micro facial expressions are subconscious; even people who are blind show these facial expressions. Micro facial expressions are like road signs. Feelings of contempt, disgust, and happiness can be easily observed by looking at someone's facial expression. And the smile is a universal positive signal. Everybody smiles the same. For a smile to be considered genuine, it must develop over three seconds and be sustained for three seconds. A half-smile or a smile which lasts less than six seconds gives insufficient data to the primitive brain of your customer and by default signals something negative.

Art of Conversation on the Telephone

Making appointments through the effective use of the telephone can save you a lot of time and also be cost-effective. Imagine trying to meet your prospect without an appointment. You travel the long distance to reach your prospect's office and then you come to find out that she is not in the office – and is not the decision maker.

Also, by calling your prospect at one geographical location, you can make appointments with all your prospects whose offices are nearby. Just by using this technique, you can save lot of travelling time and gain the ability to meet more prospects during your workday.

Sometimes salespeople are not able to talk to a prospect directly, as the phone is answered by a secretary whose job it is to ensure that the boss meets only with those he or she wants or needs to see.

If the secretary asks, "What is this about?", you should reply with something like, "I would like to speak to Mr XYZ about the new machinery he is planning to purchase." There is a good chance that the secretary will then transfer the call to his or her boss.

While speaking to the secretary, clearly mention your name and your company's name. You should impress the secretary by being pleasant and courteous. Always ask the secretary for his or her email address and the email address of your prospect during your conversation. Once you make your point about why you are calling, remain silent for a few seconds. Your silence will put pressure on the secretary. He or she will connect to your prospect.

After the appointment is fixed, immediately confirm by directly emailing your prospect. Don't forget to copy the secretary. Never send a confirmation email unless and until the prospect confirms the appointment by phone and you have agreed on a place and time for a face-to-face meeting. On the day of the meeting, call the secretary, remind him or her of your confirmation email, and request that he or she remind your prospect of the appointment. This method works well, especially if it is your first appointment with the prospect.

Important Ideas for Effective Telephone Skills:

1. Fix a specific time every day to make your phone calls, preferably towards the evening. In the morning, your prospects are likely very busy dealing with their most important jobs. Calling at the right time increases your chance of talking to decision makers. Make sure you only make presentations to the decision maker. I personally prefer to call prospects between 4 p.m. and 5:45 p.m., because in the United Arab Emirates, most offices close at 6 p.m.
2. Have clear goals for daily telephonic calls. I used to call at least twelve prospects daily, and the day after making the calls, I tried to meet at least three prospects face-to-face. Your voice should be pleasant, with your positive attitude reflecting in your tone. Your confidence and belief in your products should be reflected in your voice. Be confident but polite.
3. Speak at moderate speed so that you can communicate effectively to your prospect. Make sure you pronounce people's names correctly. Always address people by their title, e.g. Mr or Ms.
4. Always make note of your conversation in your diary. This helps you in follow-up. Also, when you want to recall whom you called some days back, you can refer easily to your diary. Personally I prefer to log all of my visits and telephonic calls in my daily agenda report. It helps me a lot in follow-up. The daily agenda report is discussed in detail in Chapter 18 – Time Management.

Art of Writing Letters and Emails

Start with a very strong opening line, making it an announcement. The following points are also very important when writing letters/ emails:

1. Focus on one major idea at a time. Be specific. Keep your letters short and simple, preferably half a page. It is best not to exceed one page unless totally necessary. Write short paragraphs both for openers and closers. Go with a logical sequence. Use bullet points to emphasize benefits. I personally prefer three paragraphs, which includes one short opening paragraph and one short closing paragraph.
2. Use testimonials to increase credibility of your product or service. Give prospects a strong reason to talk to you or see you. Don't promise something that you cannot deliver. Include a brochure, as it provides more information to your prospect about your product or service.
3. Always proofread and spell check carefully.
4. Close your letter with a call to action, either on your prospect's part or your part, for example, "Please acknowledge this letter" or "I shall call you within three to five days from now." Allow some breathing time before the follow-up.

CHAPTER 9

Art of Dealing with Customers

The fastest way to improve your relationships is to make others feel important in every way possible. The more you make others feel important in your presence, the more other people will like you and listen to you. To be a good sales professional, you need to develop the soft skills mentioned below.

1. **Smile**. Always meet with your customers with a smile. When you smile with happiness, then your customers feel important and valuable. They will like you. People listen to people whom they like.
2. **Thank people**. You can show your appreciation by saying "thank you" on every occasion, for any reason, small or large. You can make habit of saying "thank you" to everyone you encounter for everything they do.
3. **Express sincere and honest admiration**. Expressing your sincere and honest admiration often makes your customers feel wonderful about themselves. When you express your admiration of them, they will perceive you as more interesting and more likeable. But beware of flattery. Appreciation is sincere, whereas flattery is insincere. Appreciation is universally admired, whereas flattery is universally condemned.

4. **Pay attention.** This is the most powerful thing you can do to build rapport. When you pay close attention to others, they feel valuable and important. When someone begins talking to you, you should immediately discontinue all other activities and give that person your entire attention. Listen to what the person is saying, and then pause for a moment before replying. This shows that you actually heard the person, not only what was said but also what was meant.

Art of Dealing with Angry Customers

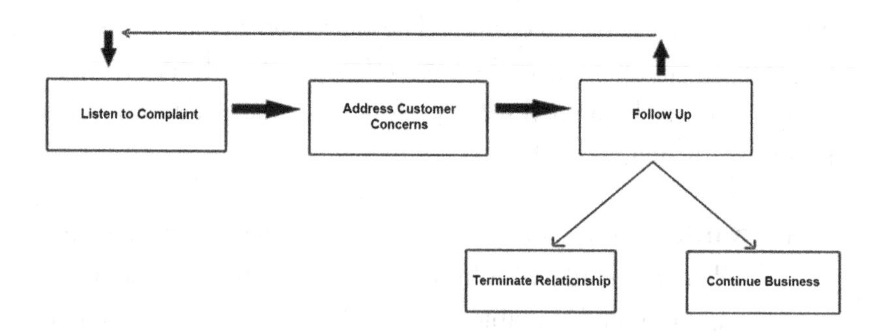

Whenever you face an angry customer, the first thing you should do is to remain calm. You have to control your urge to yell back at the person. Keep in mind that the customer is not upset with you. He is upset with the product or service. Always remember that it is professional to be far less emotional.

Listen to the angry customer's complaints patiently, because the problem cannot be solved when the customer is angry. Try to understand the root cause of the problem. If your customer is getting abusive and you find it very difficult to handle the situation, then involve your superior, as those above you are more skilled at and experienced with handling that kind of situation.

If the mistake is the customer's, for example an application mistake or the result of product mishandling, then very politely educate the customer and explain to her the reason for the product failure.

Once, I sold two light towers to a customer. The light towers my company sold were from a reputed brand and equipped with a Japanese-made engine. My company offered a warranty term of two years or four thousand running hours, as we were confident of the quality of our light towers. The customer to whom I sold the two light towers was very angry. After I listened patiently and came to understand the reason why he was upset, I promised I would send our technician to his site. Our technician informed me that the diesel engine had run 900 hours beyond the first free service performed at 250 hours. Service was again to be performed at 500 hours and 750 hours. I explained the root cause of the failure of the light towers, namely negligence to maintain the light towers at the construction site. Although it was the customer's mistake, my company repaired the light towers and returned them to the customer. Yes, we charged a fee for service and charged for the parts, but we gave the customer a special discount. The next year, the same customer purchased two more light towers from us for one of his construction sites.

On the other hand, if the problem causing a customer's anger is from your side, such as a product malfunction or negligence in service, then the first thing you should do is to apologize to your customer. Once I sold an 800 cfm diesel compressor to one of our valuable customers. Within five working hours, excessive noise started coming from the compressor. The customer called me and was very angry. For ten minutes I listened patiently. After I understood his complaint, I promised that I would send our technician to his worksite that day to check the compressor. Our technician determined that the noise coming from the compressor was unusual, so we advised him to bring the compressor back to our workshop. I called the customer on the telephone, apologized, and assured him of a solution. Then I discussed the matter with my service manager, the head of sales, and finally our principal. The final decision was to repair the faulty compressor free of charge. Since we were transparent in our communication with the customer and since we took a proactive approach, that customer gave us repeat business after some months.

During the sale, it is generally the salesperson who calls the customer every time, but when there is a problem, it is generally the customer who calls the salesperson to complain. By properly handling a customer's complaint, you not only retain that customer but also receive repeat business in future. Customer complaints should be given top priority. Your customer's negative perception needs to be corrected as soon as possible, convincingly, and in a polite manner.

KEEP COOL IN THE FACE OF YOUR MOST DIFFICULT CUSTOMERS

CHAPTER 10

Importance of Continuous Education

> Continuous learning is the minimum requirement for success in any field.
>
> Denis Waitley

> Anyone who stops learning is old, whether twenty or eighty. Anyone who keeps learning stays young. The greatest thing you can do is keep your mind young.
>
> Mark Twain

A person who graduated yesterday and stops learning today is uneducated by tomorrow. Never stop learning, because life never stops teaching. We don't have the luxury of learning every life lessons by way of our own experience. Therefore, it is helpful to learn from the experiences of others. We learn in two ways: by reading and by associating with smart people. Our real learning starts after we finish our college education. Very few people read once they get a job, as they cease trying to improve themselves, which means that they fail to rise above mediocrity. Top sales professionals, on the other hand, regularly attend continuing improvement programmes in order to excel in their field. You should develop the habit of reading material related to your products and to sales skills, and so forth, each day, at least half an hour before going in to work.

There is famous story that tells of the importance of continuing education. A certain woodcutter had worked for a company for five years but had never gotten a pay rise. The company hired a new person, and within a year that person was given an increase in salary. This caused the woodcutter to become angry and bitter, as he had been working there longer. He went to his supervisor and asked, "Why did the new person get a salary increase when I haven't gotten a pay rise in the last five years?"

The supervisor said, "We are a results-oriented company. The new guy's output went up, so he got a raise. Your output hasn't increased in the last five years."

So the man went back to work. He started hitting harder with the axe and putting in more hours, but his output remained the same. He thought to himself that maybe the new person knew some special technique. He went and asked him about the secret of his success.

The newer employee said, "After cutting every tree, I take a break for two minutes and sharpen my axe. When was the last time you sharpened your axe?"

The woodcutter said, "Oh, five years ago!"

This story says it all. Continuing education is like sharpening your axe. Good sales professionals are always engaged in a continuing education programme in order to sharpen their sales skills. You should learn more if you want to earn more.

Focus to sharpen your sales skills daily, spending at least half an hour reading material related to sales and practising your techniques each day. If you do this, then soon you will be a genius at sales. The formula to become genius is to focus and to spend time each day improving your skills. Understand this formula deeply and act on it. If you do, then within three to five years, you will be a very successful sales professional. Others will treat you as a genius of your field. Your life will never be the same. As entrepreneur Jim Rohn said, "Formal education will make you a living, self education will make you a fortune."

Following are some common reasons why salespeople fail to get orders from customers:

- failure to practice their sales presentation
- lack of knowledge about the product being sold
- lack of knowledge about the market and the competition
- lack of sales skills.

Reading is the eye of the mind. When you read more about selling, you learn new ideas to sell more of your products. The more you read, the faster you move to the top of your field. Develop your own library of sales books. Each morning, instead of reading the newspaper or watching television, spend thirty to sixty minutes reading something on sales that will help you to perform better during the day. What you put into your mind in the first hour after rising sets the tone of your mind for the rest of the day. If you feed your mind with something positive, educational, and uplifting in that first hour, then you will perform better all day long. You will be more flexible and confident. Also, you will bounce back faster from rejection and disappointment if you start your day with a dose of motivation.

Business speaker Nick Carter once said, "Audio learning is the greatest breakthrough in education since the invention of the printing press." By turning your car into a learning machine, that is by listening audiobooks and podcasts, you will be astonished at the enormous number of great ideas you will hear on daily basis. As Zig Ziglar said, "Enroll in automobile university and attend full time for the rest of your career." Turn your travelling time into learning time.

Small daily improvements over time lead to stunning results. When during your reading or listening you discover a new sales skill or hear new information, think on it until you understand the concept clearly, and then apply that skill and information during your working hours. If the idea or technique works, then continue to hone that skill. If it doesn't work, then keep on learning new skills and ideas. The ability to think and to learn is one of the biggest advantages we humans have over all other living creatures. Confucius said, "He who learns but does not think is lost. He who thinks but does not learn is in great danger."

If you are not willing to learn, then no one can help you. If you are determined to learn, then no one can stop you. The capacity to learn is a gift, the ability to learn is a skill, and the willingness to learn is a choice. So remain curious and keep learning. Always remember that the expert was once a beginner. What we learn becomes a part of who we are. If you want to earn more, then you will have to learn more.

One research study found that successful professionals exhibited the following six traits:

1. intelligence
2. diligence (willingness to work hard)
3. obedience

4. passion
5. willingness to take initiative
6. innovation.

The first three traits are the minimum requirement to succeed in today's competitive environment. The last three traits are the cutting edge that make you different from the average sales professional. To develop these traits, you have to remain always in learning mode. We learn by reading books (or listening to audiobooks) and associating with smarter people. The novelist George R. R. Martin said, "A reader lives a thousand lives before he dies, The Man who never reads lives only one."

> He who learns but does not think is lost!
> He who thinks but does not learn is in great danger.
>
> Confucius

> The capacity to learn is a gift; the ability to learn is a skill; the willingness to learn is a choice.
>
> Brian Herbert

CHAPTER 11

Selling Is Both an Art and a Science

Selling is an art in the sense that the salesperson is dealing with human beings, who are unpredictable. Human beings are emotional creatures, and every one of them is unique. Selling is also a science because by following a certain series of steps in sequence, a salesperson's closing ratio and probability of making the sale become much higher. Selling is based on a certain principle that if repeated will produce the same or a similar result.

The following things are what the best salespeople sell (in order):

1. themselves
2. their company
3. their service or product
4. price.

The following things are what ordinary salespeople sell (in order):

1. price
2. their service or product
3. their company
4. themselves.

A professional salesperson does the following things:

1. creates new customers and retains existing customers;
2. generates new business from existing customers as well as new customers;
3. establishes a relationship of trust, building credibility and goodwill, with customers;
4. becomes a point of contact for all of his customers, helping them become more productive and profitable;
5. acts as a source of feedback and market information to her company.

Give Your Customer at Least Three Reasons to Purchase What You Are Selling

Find at least three strong reasons for the customer to make the purchase decision in your favour. Following are some examples of such reasons:

1. a better price performance ratio versus the competitor's product or service
2. better after-sale and service support than the competition
3. better parts availability
4. better warranty terms.
5. better quality and better specifications.

Each time you describe a benefit in your sales presentation, your prospect's desire to purchase what you're selling increases. The more logical and pre-planned your presentation is, the faster and more easily you will be able to sell.

The Major Reasons Customers Don't Buy

- Fear of failure is one of the major reasons why customers don't buy. Customers may be especially fearful of buying from you if the brand you are offering is new to the market or if they have never purchased your type of product before. In such cases, customers are fearful of paying too much or of being criticized for making the wrong choice. To sell any customer the first few products is always challenging, especially if the product you are offering is new to him. Once you have some reference letters from satisfied customers, you should share these with prospects to help them overcome their fear of failure. As a salesperson, you must not only stimulate a prospect's desire to buy your product but also help your prospect overcome all the fears related to his decision to buy your product or service. To sell the first few units, you can, with approval from your suppliers and sales head, offer some additional benefits to help your customer overcome the fear of failure. When my company launched the light tower, it was a product new to the market. The standard warranty term for the competitor's similar product was one year or two thousand hours. We offered a warranty of two or four thousand hours, and we positioned our light towers' price in line with our competitor's similar offering. This strategy helped us to sell the first few units in the initial phase after product launch. Once we have reference letters from customers who were satisfied with our light towers, it was easy to convince new customers to buy.
- Another major reason why a customer does not buy your product or service is human inertia. If a prospect is comfortable using a particular brand of product or service, it is much easier for her to continue with what she is doing

than to make a change. To get a prospect to change from her current product or service to your offering, you must highlight all the additional benefits that she will enjoy. The attractiveness of the benefits must be so great that they motivate the prospect to make the change from her existing product or services. With better warranty terms, better after-sales service, or unique product features, you can convince your prospect to use your product in place of the competitor's product.

- Sometimes you find that in spite of visiting a prospect and communicating often with him, you are unable to develop a bond because your prospect is on a different wavelength than you are. In such a case, you should suggest that a colleague on your sales team, one who would probably get along better with the prospect, take the account. It is nearly impossible to sell to a prospect you don't like.

Do's and Don'ts of Selling

Do's:

- Use testimonial letters from your satisfied customers. Sharing letters of testimony from your satisfied customers with new prospects is a powerful way to convince the latter to buy what you are selling. Along with testimonial letters, you can ask permission from your satisfied customers to share their telephone number with your prospects. Once I was negotiating a big deal with a rental company, attempting to sell them twenty-five walk-behind rollers. During discussion after my presentation and after overcoming all of the prospect's objections related to my offer, I informed the prospect that some months back I had sold a large quantity of these rollers to another rental company. I shared that customer's contact information with my prospect, as the latter knew the former very well. Once the two talked, my prospect was convinced. I got the order.

- After you have presented or demonstrated, you must convincingly reply to all the prospect's major objections. You have to use the art of objection handling convincingly and prepare the ground for the next and most important step: asking to close the order.
- Meet the obligation you have to your customers by moving smoothly through the close and ensuring that the process is as quick and painless as possible. You need to practise the art of closing.
- Observe a brief period of silence after you ask the closing question. The only pressure that you should apply as a sales professional is the pressure of this silence.

Don'ts:

- Never offer your product or service without understanding the need of customer. After you understand correctly the need of your prospect, then you should start presenting the product or service which best suited to that customer's need.
- Never tell the prospect that he is wrong. Never argue with him. As said by Dale Carnegie, "If a man convinced against his will, then he will remain at his opinion still." The prospect is always right.
- Avoid the subjects of religion, politics, and sex. You can nod and agree with the prospect's opinion, but don't feed the fire by adding comments of your own. Instead, gently bring the conversation back around to your product or service by asking questions related to it. Keep your opinion to yourself.
- Never criticize your competitors. If a prospect asks you about competitor, say, XYZ Company, then you can say

something like, "XYZ is an excellent company. They have good products, and they have been around for a long time. However, we believe that our product is superior to XYZ's." Inform your prospect of the major competitive advantage of your products or service.

- Avoid making promises to your prospect that you can't keep. Never oversell your product by saying that your product can do something that it cannot do. Never lie to your customer.
- Never disclose the price before you explain the values and benefit of your product or service. First develop the buying desire, and then reveal the price.

CHAPTER 12

Art of Objection Handling

There are no sales without objections. Objections indicate interest. If there is no interest, there will be no sale. Objections are signposts that lead you step by step towards closing the sale. The more objections you get, the more likely it is that you are moving towards actually making the sale. The very best salespeople are those who have learned to deal with objections in the fastest and most effective way.

Reply to customer objections in two stages: (1) reassure your customer, and (2) reinforce your position.

While answering objection, you have to not only reassure your customers but also reinforce your position about the product or service you are trying to sell. For example:

- We sell a lot of this product and our price is very competitive.
- Our customers are extremely satisfied, and the quality of our product is proven.
- This model is our most popular model, and the price–performance ratio is excellent for this model of product versus the competitor's offering.

Table 12.1 **Common customer objections, and responses to them**

Most customers' objections can be classified as one of the six mentioned in Table 12.1.

Customer objection	Your response
Price	"Our price is in line with our competitors' prices." (The comparison must be fair, i.e. comparing apples to apples.)
Quality	"The quality of our product is equal to or better than our competitor's product."
Competitor offering	"We have a competitive advantage." (Then mention the advantage, e.g. better after-sales support, better warranty terms, better parts availability versus the competition.)
Capability	"Allow me to give you a product demonstration."
Reputation	"Here are some testimonial letters for you to read."
Newness	"We are offering a special promotion for the first few units you buy."

Your job is to develop a convincing answer for each of your prospect's major objections. Whatever you need to do to eliminate these major objections, start doing it immediately, addressing each matter in terms of its priority. Keep in mind that the price–performance ratio must be in line with similar products offered by your competitors. For example, if you are selling Pepsi Cola, then you cannot charge more than Coca-Cola, and at the same time your product's quality must be in line with the quality of Coca-Cola.

One of the most powerful ways to eliminate objections is to present testimonial letters written by your satisfied customers.

If your customer raises an objection after you finish your presentation or product demonstration, then treat the objection as a request for more information. Objecting is a natural customer response to any offering when there is some risk related to the purchase.

Table 12.2 **Common customer objections, and what they actually mean**

What the customer says as an objection	What he or she actually means
"The price is too high."	"Convince me that your price-to-performance ratio is best and that I will get more value from purchasing your product [or service]."
"A similar product is available from one of your competitors at a lower price."	"Inform me of the competitive advantages and the value I will receive after I purchase this product [or service] from you and not from the competition."
"I can't afford it."	"Help me justify the expense of purchasing your product [or service]."
"I have to talk with someone else before deciding."	"Provide me with sufficient reason to buy from you so that I don't have to get someone else's opinion."

"I will call you back."	"Provide me with more information so that I can take my decision now."

Table 12.3 **The feel, felt, and found method**

The feel, felt, and found method is a professional way of acknowledging the prospect's objection as being valid, assuring the prospect that she is not alone in her concern, and then answering her objection in a satisfactory way.

What the customer says as an objection	**Your reply using the feel, felt, and found method**
"The price is too high."	"I understand exactly how you feel. Others felt the same way when I first spoke to them, But this is what they found." Then explain that others who had same concern are now very happy with their decision, as they got much more in value from buying from you.
"A similar product is available from your competitor for a lower price."	"I understand exactly how you feel. Others felt the same way when I first spoke to them, But this is what they found." Then enumerate the competitive advantages of your product or service. Inform the prospect that those customers who had same concern are now very happy with their decision, as they got much more in value from buying from you.

"I can't afford it."	"I understand exactly how you feel. Others felt the same way when I first spoke to them, But this is what they found." Then explain the values and benefits of your product or service. Inform the prospect that those customers who said the same are now very happy with their decision, as they got much more in value from buying from you.

Whenever possible, provide proof for your answer in the form of a testimonial letter, a price comparison, or even a magazine or newspaper article attesting to the quality of your product or service.

After you answer the prospect's objection, don't forget to ask, "Does this answer your question?"

CHAPTER 13

Art of Closing the Sale

There are three things you must be sure of before you go to close the sale. They are:

1. The prospect has a need for your product or service.
2. The prospect is able to afford your product or service.
3. The prospect is able to use your product or service.

If you ask for the prospect's order before these three things have been determined, you will not able to close the sale.

Recognizing Buying Signals

There are several common buying signals that the prospect will give once he has made up his mind to buy what you are selling. Relax and try to recognize those buying signals. Remember the old adage "Strike while the iron is hot." The right time to ask the closing question is once you recognize the buying signals from your prospect.

Sudden Friendliness

When your prospect has made up her mind to buy from you, then she will seem to relax and become happy. She will seem suddenly friendly and may ask you a personal question, for example: "How many kids do you have? In which school they are studying?"; "Would you like another cup of tea?"; "In which area do you reside?" Any noticeable change in attitude, posture, or voice can indicate that a buying decision has been made.

Whenever you experience this sudden friendliness, you should respond warmly and positively and then ask the closing question. For example:

- "Thank you. I am blessed with two kids. They are studying in Sharjah Indian School. By the way, at which of your locations do you prefer to take delivery?"
- "Thank you. I will have another cup of tea. And by the way, how soon will you need this product?"

Chin Rubbing

Chin rubbing is another sign that the customer has approached a buying decision. When the prospect's hand comes down from his chin, you should smile and ask a closing question, such as, "How soon do you need this?" Then sit silently until you get confirmation.

Asking Questions about Price, Terms, or Delivery

The most common buying signal is when the prospect asks you about price, payment terms, or delivery. Whenever the prospect asks you a question involving price, payment terms, or delivery, turn it into a closing question by asking about one of the three subjects the prospect did not mention.

For example, when the prospect asks, "What will be the payment terms?", you should reply, "How soon do you need the product delivered?"

When the prospect says, "By the end of the month," then the sale is made. After hearing this, you should explain the payment methods your company accepts, such as cash, current dated cheques (CDC), or postdated cheques (PDC).

Remember that the person who asks questions has control. This is key. Therefore, always try to answer a question with a question.

Closing is the most difficult stage of the selling process for the salesperson. Three of the most common reasons for this are:

1. the salesperson's fear of rejection
2. the salesperson's fear of failure
3. the salesperson's lack of enthusiasm.

Fear of Rejection

Salespeople have natural fear of rejection, as no one wants to hear no. Note, however, that when a prospect says, "I am not interested," she is rejecting not you but the product or service which you are offering. As a successful salesperson, you must be very clear in your mind that *rejection is not personal*. Professionals are always less emotional. *No* means "next opportunity."

Fear of Failure

The second main reason that closing is hard is because the salesperson fears failure. You fear that you will have wasted your time, your effort, and your energy if the prospect decides not to buy from you.

The fear of failure, coupled with the fear of rejection, is the primary reason people underachieve or fail in life. It is only when you get over these two fears that you begin to realize your full potential in sales, and in every other area of your life.

Keep reminding yourself that there is no such thing as failure; there is only feedback. Ralph Waldo Emerson wrote, "Do the thing you fear and the death of fear is certain." The only way that you can eliminate a fear that might be holding you back is to do the thing that you fear.

Another major obstacle to closing the sale is negative expectation. This occur when the salesperson decides in advance that a particular prospect is not going to buy. The salesperson jumps to the conclusion that this is not a good prospect and stops making any real effort to conclude the sale.

Lack of Enthusiasm

This is another major barrier to closing the sale. *Selling is the transfer of enthusiasm from the seller to the buyer.* If the salesperson is not enthusiastic about selling, then he will find it almost impossible to close the sale.

To succeed in selling, you must have energy. You must really want to close sales. You must feel strongly that what you are selling is truly advantageous for your customer. You must have ambition and a strong desire to be a very successful sales professional.

Some Popular and Proven Closing Techniques

- **The secondary close/trial close**

  A good sales professional, before closing, does a trial close. A trial close gives the salesperson an indication as to how close she is to the point where it is appropriate to ask for the order. A trial close seeks the prospect's opinion, whereas the final close asks for the prospect's decision. The trial close involves closing on a minor point made in the sales presentation. If the prospect agrees to the minor point, then he has, by extension, decided to buy the entire offer.

  For example, if a prospect is considering buying a refrigerator, you initiate the trial close by asking, "Would you prefer this in red or white?" The colour is a secondary issue. The purchase is the major issue. If the prospect says that he would prefer it in red, then he has decided to buy the refrigerator.

  Another way to use the trial close is to ask, "Would you like this delivered, or will you arrange delivery yourself?" How the prospect prefers to take delivery is the secondary issue. But by saying that he wants the item delivered to his home, he is indicating that he has made the decision to buy.

- **Satisfying the final objection.**

  You say to your prospect, "If I could answer your objection to your complete satisfaction, would you be prepared to go ahead with this purchase?" Remain silent and wait for her to answer.

When the prospect finally says, "Yes, if you can answer it, then I will be ready to make a buying decision," you should follow up with this question: "What would it take to satisfy you on this point?" And then again, wait silently for your prospect to give you the "closing condition."

You then go ahead and show her that you can answer this objection to her complete satisfaction. Once you have satisfied the prospect, you should ask for her order.

❖ **The "just suppose" close**

The prospect says, "I am sorry. I like what you have shown me, but we have decided to go for a rental option in place of buying your equipment." You answer, "Mr Prospect, just suppose that was not a problem. Is there any other reason that would cause you to hesitate about going ahead right now?" When you phrase things in this way, the prospect has to say, "No, that's the only reason," or "Well, there is another reason."

You can then uncover the final reason and close the sale. For example: "Just suppose we could provide better payment terms, for example 12 PDC. The price of a 24-ton crawler excavator is 360,000 dirhams [the currency of the United Arab Emirates]. The monthly rental charge is 15,000 dirhams. If you agree to pay with 12 postdated cheques, then it means you will pay 30,000 dirhams every month for one year and will recover your investment cost. Just suppose I could get approval for this better payment option from our management and get back to you tomorrow."

❖ **The sharp-angle close**

You close on the prospect's objection. Sometimes this method is called the bear trap close or the porcupine close.

It is very effective when the customer has almost run out of objections or buying resistance.

The prospect says, "I can't afford the monthly payments." You reply, "If we could spread the payments over an extra year, would you take the deal?"

The prospect might say, "Your product won't perform to my specifications." You respond, "If we could demonstrate to you that it will, would you take the deal?"

- **The instant reverse close**

  When the prospect gives you any objection at all, especially a standard, well-used objection such as "We can't afford it," you should answer, "Mr Prospect, that's exactly why you should take it, because you can't afford it." This always grabs the prospect's attention and forces him to ask, "What? What do you mean?" Then you reply, "Mr Prospect, that's exactly why you should take it today at this price, because you will never get a better combination of product, quality, and price as you are getting right now. Why don't you take it?"

- **The change-places close**

  When you have not been able to uncover your prospect's key objection, you can use the change-places close. This is especially effective when the prospect will not give you a straight answer.

  You have established a friendly relationship and given your presentation, but the prospect still won't tell you what she is thinking. You say, "Ms Prospect, let's change places for just a minute. Put yourself in my situation and imagine you were me. Imagine you are talking to someone whom you respect. You have shown him an excellent product and yet he won't make a decision one way or another, and he won't give you reason why. What would you do or say if you were in my shoes?" There is very good chance that the prospect will then reveal the real reason for her hesitation to go ahead with your offer.

- **The Ben Franklin close**
  This is one of the oldest closing techniques. It was developed by the American statesman, inventor, and diplomat Ben Franklin in 1765. Franklin used to take a piece of paper and draw a line down the centre before making any complex decision. On one side of the line he would write all the reasons in favour of the decision, and on the other side he would write all the reasons opposed to the decision. When using the Ben Franklin close, you do the same thing, writing all ten reasons in favour to the decision. Explain the concept to your prospect and then give him the paper so he can write down the reasons he has against placing order with you. Most prospects can think of only one or two reasons for not buying your product or service. You then compare these reasons against the ten reasons you provided in favour of the decision. As a note of caution, one disadvantage may be more significant than ten advantages.

- **The invitational close**
  At the end of your sales presentation, you simply issue a direct invitation to the prospect to buy what you have just described.

  First you ask, "Do you like what I have shown you so far?" When the prospect says, "Yes," then you immediately ask, "Well then, why don't you give it a try?"

- **Dealing with price resistance**

  You must spend a good deal of time building the value of your product or service before you even mention price. Your goal is to increase the prospect's willingness to pay by building buying desire. Repeating and highlighting the benefits that your prospect will enjoy from your product or service will accomplish this goal. Convince the prospect that the value of your product is far greater than the cost. *First talk about the benefits, and only then reveal the price. This is a fundamental rule in selling.* Do not bring up price at the beginning of your talk, under any circumstances. Increase buying desire by highlighting benefits. You do not increase buying desire by arguing about the price.

- **The sandwich close**

  When the time has finally come to address the question of price, don't simply tell a prospect the number of dirhams. Instead, use what is called the sandwich close. With this close, you sandwich the price between two benefits the customer will enjoy from your product or service. Say for example that you are selling a backhoe loader. After you finish your presentation, the prospect asks about the price. You can say, "This machine includes a two-year warranty. It has an extended arm and a clamshell bucket, and will cost you 225,000 dirhams."

- **Compare apples to apples**

  Always compare apples to apples and oranges to oranges. Find out what your competitors are charging for what you sell, and discover the reason for any price difference. Say for example you are selling a 100-kVA diesel generator and you tell your prospect that it will cost him 50,000 dirhams. If the prospect replies, "It's very high price," you then ask, "Compared with what?" If the prospect is comparing your branded diesel generator with a generator manufactured in the UAE, then of course the price of yours will be much higher. Then you explain to the prospect why your branded diesel generator is more expensive than the locally fabricated generator.

Willingness to pay and ability to pay are two different things. Most people can buy a product or service if they are willing to pay. Your goal is to increase the prospect's willingness to pay by building her buying desire. Convince your prospect that the value of your product is far greater than the cost. She must be fully convinced that the advantages she will receive are greater than what she is going to pay for your product or service.

❖ **The reverse close**

Here the sales professional asks questions to eliminate the prospect's objections. Every elimination of a negative brings you closer to the positive. Examples of some questions to ask are:

> Is it my credibility that bothers you?
>
> Is it my company's credibility that bothers you?
>
> Is it that you think the product is not good?

Every no the prospect says eliminates a negative and brings you closer to a positive close.

❖ **The silence close**

After your presentation, and once you successfully handle all of your prospect's objections, you ask a closing question.

Once you ask the closing question, you must be silent but maintain eye contact without staring. Your silence puts a great deal of pressure on the prospect. Now the prospect has no choice but to make a decision.

CHAPTER 14

Sales Strategy

> If you do not have a strategy, you become a part of someone else strategy.
>
> Alvin Toffler

> If the rate of change on the outside exceeds the rate of change on the inside of your company, then end is near.
>
> Jack Welch

Strategy is the central, integrated, externally oriented concept of how a business will achieve its objectives in a way that gives competitive advantage and sustainable superior returns. A *sales strategy* is a comprehensive plan to get customers to purchase your products and services. While it can be based on your marketing and business strategies, a sales strategy focuses on making the sale rather than on increasing the visibility of your company. It's important to take the time to create a different sales strategy for each of your product lines.

Align Sales and Marketing Activities to the Customer

Marketing and sales activities should be designed to fit the customer's buying process. Find a way to integrate sharing customer information between sales and marketing team members to gain valuable insights and to enhance the customer experience. Designing sales and marketing strategies around the customer allows you to focus on identifying customer needs and finding a better way to satisfy them.

The elements of a successful sales strategy include:

- A display of importance

  Find a way to showcase the value your product or service offers to customers by explaining how it can make their lives better.

- An explanation of why you're the best

  There's a good chance that another business offers either the same product or service or one very similar to yours, so it's important to highlight the competitive advantage you have against competitors.

It is important to understand how customers make decisions associated with their purchases. Customer behaviour is influenced by numerous factors, including psychological factors, social factors, and economic factors. Having an understanding of the impact and influence of these factors helps sales professionals understand customers' purchasing behaviour.

It costs five times more money to create a new customer than to retain an existing one. It is very important to retain your existing customers and get repeat business from them. Customer satisfaction surveys are very useful to get feedback from customers. Customer satisfaction can be enhanced by:

- ❖ aligning your product or service with the need of the customer
- ❖ improving performance on a regular basis in light of availability, response time, after-sales support, etc.

The following are things to consider when aligning your product to the needs of your customers.

Product life cycle: A product goes through various stages in its life, starting from an introduction stage and continuing through to maturity and decline. Different stages generate different revenue and profits depending on the sales strategies and sales plan adopted. As a good sales professional, you must have a clear idea of the life cycle stage of the product you are selling.

Product portfolio analysis: There are various ways of managing a range of products. The simplest way is by applying Pareto's law, identifying the 20 per cent of your products which produce 80 per cent of your total profit.

SWOT analysis: The acronym SWOT stands for "strengths, weaknesses, opportunities, and threats." The SWOT analysis, which has been explained by marketing experts Igor Ansoff and Philip Kotler, involves analysing the strengths, weaknesses, opportunities, and threats facing a business. In order to succeed, a sales professional must know the strengths of his company and where it is vulnerable. SWOT analysis is very useful to the salesperson seeking to take advantage of opportunities in the marketplace and to face the challenges from competitors and the outside environment.

Strengths

A look at the inner workings of your company should help you determine what strengths your company has in relation to its resources and capabilities, structure, culture, leadership, products, systems, values, and processes.

Weaknesses

What are the key bottlenecks in your company?

Opportunities

What opportunities do you see available to your company?

Threats

In looking outside your company, what threats do you see to your business (for example changing technology, a better product offered by a competitor, or service deficiencies)?

Strengths and weaknesses relate to factors within your company, whereas opportunities and threats relate to factors outside your company.

Porter's five forces analysis: Management guru Michael Porter developed his five forces analysis in reaction to SWOT analysis. Assessing the competitive environment involves looking at barriers to marketplace entry and exit, the availability of substitutes, bargaining power of sellers and buyers, and the intensity of the competition.

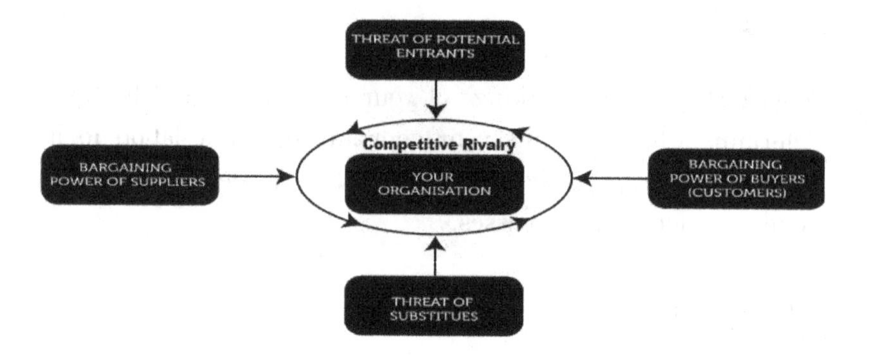

Porter's five forces include (1) the threat of substitute products or services, (2) the threat of established rivals, (3) the threat of new entrants, (4) the bargaining power of suppliers, and (5) the bargaining power of buyers/customers.

Porter's five forces analysis is a framework that attempts to analyse both the level of competition within an industry and business strategy development. It draws upon industrial organization economics to derive those five forces that determine the competitive intensity within, and therefore the attractiveness of, an industry. Attractiveness in this context refers to the overall profitability of the industry. An "unattractive" industry is one in which the combination of these five forces acts to drive down overall profitability.

A successful salesperson regularly asks the following questions of himself. If he finds himself deficient in one or more of the basic components, he must communicate this to his marketing department and management team. For any company, the salespeople are the eyes and ears, so it is their responsibility to communicate any important information about the market which they receive. As business executive Jack Welch said, "If rate of change in outside is more than rate of change inside then your change is in sight."

1. Is the product quality is in line with the competition?
2. Who are the major competitors, and what is their market share?
3. Is the product priced right compared to similar competitive products on the market?
4. What are the competitive advantages of my product or services and also of my company?
5. Is my market is underserved or overserved?
6. What is the market size for my targeted product or service? How much of the market share does my company currently have? How much market share are we seeking to gain?
7. How is my product or service positioned – as leader or follower, or as a challenger – in the market?
8. Is my after-sales service is in line with the competition's?

The purpose of any business is to make money now and in future. The main objective of a salesperson is to convert inventory into cash with a profitable margin. The successful salesperson always tries to increase the return on assets or inventory. She knows that return on inventory is the product of margin and inventory turnover. Money-making in business has three basic components: cash generation, return on assets, and growth. Add customers to these three parts of money-making and you have the core, or nucleus, of any business.

Following are questions to ask about your company to determine its success:

1. Does the business generate enough cash? Are accounts receivable paid within the time frame given to customers?
2. Is the return on assets in line with the industry average? Is the business growing? What were the sales during the previous year?

3. Are margins and inventory turnover in line with the industry average?
4. Are we retaining customers? Are we generating new customers?
5. Are our sales gaining, or are we losing business to the competition?

Customers need a simple reason to buy from you. You have to give them something they really need or want. What customers are buying includes the salesperson's and seller's trustworthiness.

It is very important to know the market size of the product or service you are selling. It is also very important to know about are all the active competitors, along with their market share. What is the current supply and demand situation in the market? How is the market performing? Is business booming, in recession, or normal? What is the inventory situation of all your competitors? Is there a scarcity of supply, a flood of supply, or a normal supply? Are there any threats, such as new entrants or substitute products? All this information will surely help you to understand whether your target market is attractive or not. If it is attractive, then you will have to determine how you will take market share away from the competition and how the market size can be increased for your product or service. You must know your current market share of your product or service and then implement a strategy to reach your goal of increasing that market share.

The market is changing, so businesses must change or else become a victim of change. Jack Welch aptly said, "If the rate of change on the outside exceeds the rate of change on the inside of your company, then end is near of your company."

CHAPTER 15

Marketing

> Stop pushing people to say Yes. Start asking questions that get people to think HMMM ...
>
> Mike Rodrigues

Marketing integrates all the functions of a business and speaks directly to the customers through advertising, salespeople, and other marketing activities. Marketing is an organizational function and a set of processes for creating, communicating, and delivering value to customers and managing customer relationships in ways that benefit the organization and its stakeholders. Marketing management is the art and science of choosing target markets and getting, keeping, and growing customers through creating, delivering, and communicating superior customer value in such a way that it is profitable to all of the stakeholders. The aim of marketing is to know and understand the customer so well that the product or service fits him and sells itself. One marketing concept rightly suggests that it is better to find out what the customer wants and offer that product than to make a product and then try to sell it to somebody. *As a good sales professional, you should know the marketing process.*

Selling versus Marketing

According to marketing guru Theodore Levitt, "Selling focuses on the need of the seller and marketing on the needs of the buyer. Selling is preoccupied with the seller's need to convert his product into cash. Marketing is preoccupied with the idea of satisfying the needs of the customer by means of the products and the whole cluster of things associated with creating, delivering and finally consuming it." Marketing expert advocates selling benefits to customers rather than praising the attributes of the product or service. He emphasizes that salespeople should focus on what benefits customers would gain by acquiring the product or service.

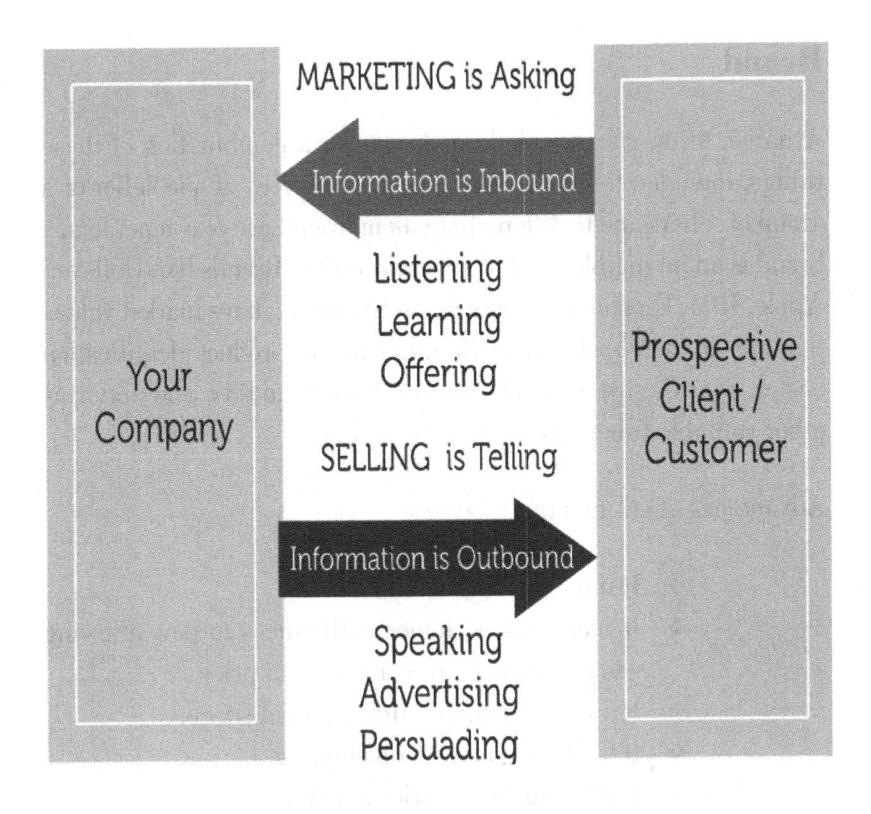
MARKETING is Asking
Information is Inbound
Listening
Learning
Offering
Your Company
Prospective Client / Customer
SELLING is Telling
Information is Outbound
Speaking
Advertising
Persuading

SELLING VS. MARKETING CONCEPT
FACTORY
EXISTING PRODUCTS & SERVICES
SELLING & PROMOTION
PROFITS THROUGH SALES VOLUME
SELLING
MARKET
FOCUS
MEANS
ENDS
MARKET
CUSTOMER NEEDS
INTEGRATED MARKETING
PROFITS THROUGH CUSTOMER SATISFACTION
MARKETING

Brand

A name, term, sign, symbol, or design, or a combination of these things, intended to identify the goods or services of one seller or a group of sellers and to differentiate them from those of competitors, a brand is an intangible asset of an organization. Brands like Unilever, Apple, IBM, Facebook, Microsoft, and Samsung have market values that exceed their book values. Branding makes product identification easier, assures customers of a certain level of quality, and performs other valuable functions.

Advantages of strong branding:

- It indicates high quality.
- It increases customer willingness to pay, allowing companies to charge a premium price.
- It commands marketing channel space.
- It facilitates market positioning.
- It constitutes a barrier to entry.

Brand Extension

Brand extension is a strategy by which an established brand name is applied to new products. For example, the Tata brand (known for Tata Motors and Tata Steel) is applied to salt (Tata Salt) and to the consultancy service TCS (Tata Consultancy Services).

Brand Loyalty

Customer satisfaction comes first, and is followed by loyalty. To get customers to become loyal to brands, it is important for the company to understand its customers' needs and aspirations. Then this knowledge can be leveraged to develop the brand. Loyalty cards offered by various organizations are designed to establish loyalty.

Marketing Strategy Process

Marketing strategy should be aligned with corporate strategy. A circular function, the marketing process consists of seven parts.

1. **Consumer analysis**
   All marketing plans should begin with the customer and his or her needs. The objective of consumer analysis is to identify segments or groups within a population with similar needs so that marketing efforts can be directly targeted to them. Several important questions must be asked, for example:

   - What is the need category?
   - Who is buying and who is using the product?
   - What is the buying process?
   - Is what I'm selling a high- or low-involvement product?
   - How can I segment the market?

2. **Market analysis**
   This takes a broader view of potential consumers to include market sizes and trends. Important questions to evaluate a market are:

   - What is the relevant market?
   - Where is the product in its life cycle?
   - What are the key competitive factors in the industry?

3. **Analysis of your company versus the competition**
   At this stage, you have chosen a consumer segment towards which to your efforts. Now a plan to beat the competition must be developed. Important questions to ask are:

   - What are my company's advantages? What things do we do well?
   - What are my company's weaknesses?
   - How can our company capitalize on its strengths or exploit our competitors' weaknesses?
   - How does our company's SWOT compare to our competitor's SWOT?

   SWOT, as mentioned in Chapter 14, stands for "strengths, weaknesses, opportunities, and threats." Strengths and weaknesses are internal factors; opportunities and threats are external factors.

4. **Review of the distribution channels**
   Distribution channel analysis is critical, because the choice of channel influences the price you can charge, and consequently the profit margin. Three important questions to ask about your distribution decision are as follows:

   - How can my product reach the consumer?
   - How much do the players in each distribution channel profit?
   - Who holds the power in each available distribution channel?

5. **Development of a "preliminary" marketing mix**
   Based on judgment developed during the analysis of the customer, the market, the competition, and the distribution channels, a manager makes an action plan. The manager

chooses what mix of efforts should be made. This mix is commonly referred as "the four P's of marketing," which are

- product
- place
- promotion
- price.

6. **Evaluation of the economics**
   This is the last step of a marketing analysis. To determine whether you have created a plan that is both profitable and reasonable, you must ask these questions:

   - What are the costs?
   - What is the break-even point?
   - How long is the payback of my investment?

CHAPTER 16

Segmentation, Targeting, and Positioning

After the phases of the marketing process discussed in the previous chapter, the next phase begins, which consists of the following three steps:

1. market segmentation
2. target market selection
3. positioning.

These steps are the prerequisites for designing a successful strategy. They allow you to focus your efforts on the right customers. Product positioning, in particular, provides the synergy among the four P's (product, place, price, and promotion) of the marketing plan.

Market Segmentation

Market segmentation consists of dividing the market into groups of potential customers – called market segments – with distinct characteristics, behaviours, or needs. The aim is to cluster customers into groups that clearly differ from one another but whose members show a great deal of homogeneity. As such, compared with a large, heterogeneous market, those segments can be served more efficiently with products that match their needs.

It is important that segments are sufficiently different from one another. Typically, customers are segmented based on the benefits they seek from a particular product. In summary, segmentation requires the marketer to take the following steps:

- Understand the benefits that customers seek.
- Segment the market and develop customer profiles based on the customer benefits.
- Find the observable variables most likely to discriminate among the benefit segments to identify membership in specific segments.

Target Market Selection

Once you understand the structure of consumer demand, you have to decide which segments you want to serve and how. In addition to a solid understanding of the customer, analysis of the competitive environment and the company is instrumental to the task of target market selection. The objective is to select segments in such a way that the firm maximizes profit.

Market segmentation is generally followed by differentiation. Segments are always related to customers. Differentiation, which always relates to products, involves collecting and comparing data about the company and its competitors to evaluate which is most likely to succeed in serving each of the identified segments.

Positioning

Positioning is defined as the marketer's effort to identify a unique selling proposition for the product. What I am selling to whom, and why will they buy it? A good positioning statement answers three questions:

- Who are the customers?
- What is the set of needs that the product fulfils?
- Why is the product the best option to satisfy those needs?

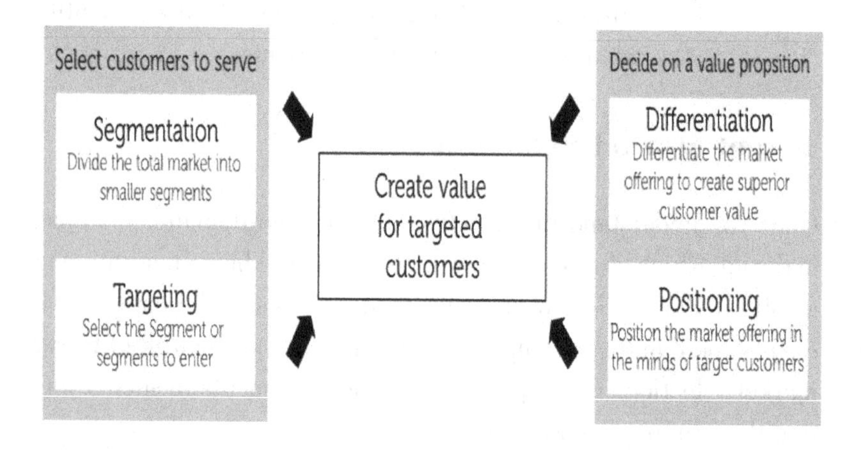

Market Segmentation
Targeting- Select the Target Market
Product Positioning
Decide on the Optimal Marketing Mix

CHAPTER 17

What Customers Love

Customers do business with people whom they like and who make them feel good. When they see that you have their best interests in mind, they will trust you. Once they know that you are good, they will be good to you. Show genuine interest in your customers. Business is all about relationships. Customers buy with their hearts. Touch the hearts of the people you serve and they will be back for more. Engage their emotions and they will be loyal customers.

Never say anything about a past customer that might be heard as criticism. Those types of statements threaten prospects and clients. They make them worry that you will criticize them too. Praise all customers – especially past ones.

Consider the Spanish proverb "Whoever gossips to you will gossip about you." Never divulge anything about a customer that may appear confidential. Protect every customer, past and present. Customers know that a person who reveals the secrets of others will reveal their secrets also.

Develop empathy towards your customers. Try to understand their needs, and accordingly suggest products which are right and suitable for their needs. Remember the famous saying first mentioned in

Chapter 1: "If you see John Jones with John Jones's eyes, then you can sell John Jones what John Jones buys."

When customers love to work with you, it means that you will get their business very regularly. If customers love you, then they will sing your praises to the world. Word of mouth is one of the most effective advertisements for your product or service. Here are some guidelines for getting customers to love working with you:

- Since customers want to stay where they are appreciated as a valued customer, establish a loyalty programme and reward your loyal customers. Good customer service entails building relationships with and providing value to your customers.
- Be genuine and transparent with your customer. You have to be genuinely interested in ensuring customer satisfaction with your offered product or service. If the customer is not happy with your service, then immediately acknowledge the problem and rectify it to his satisfaction.
- Find out how your customers perceive your company, your product, and you. If there is any negative perception, then the problem needs to be corrected immediately.
- Create opportunities for the customer to buy, rather than opportunities for you to sell.
- Have meaningful conversations with your customers. Never give them a sales pitch.
- Show curiosity about the customer as a person and let the friendship evolve from that point. Take every opportunity to thank your customers for their business. Send thank-you emails to your customers after every major purchase. Your customer surely will appreciate this.
- Believe in your heart that you and your firm are the best at what you do. Listen carefully to what your customers are

telling you. If you show you are listening and you implement the thing they have asked for, then they will love to do business with you.

- Put your customers at the heart of your business. Develop a database of your customers in Excel or other spreadsheet software your company provides for you. Keep your information up to date so as to stay close to your customers. Oftentimes a call or an email on a customer's birthday, anniversary, or other special occasion is appreciated.
- Deliver exactly what you promised to deliver, no matter what. Always deliver on time. If a problem arises, then inform the customer right away. You have to make sure that each task, from quote to delivery, is completed correctly and on time.

Customers buy products and services to help them get jobs done. As a successful salesperson, you should focus on helping the customer get her job done faster, more conveniently, and less expensively than before.

Every customer wants high-quality products, parts availability, superior technical support from competent workshop technicians/ engineers, reliable and responsible sales staff, and efficient management processes that get things done promptly and correctly. Customers want to get their job done quickly and more conveniently or less expensively. Customers want value, which is the ratio of what they get to what they pay.

The best way to ensure customer loyalty is to provide exceptional customer service and support. It is a common belief that your customers stop doing business with a company because of pricing or product offerings. That's not true. Research has found that the major reason customers leave a company is that they think the company does not care about them.

Customers want to be treated as individuals. They want to feel that their business matters to you and you care about and value them.

CHAPTER 18

Time Management

> People often complain about lack of time when the lack of direction is the real problem.
>
> Zig Ziglar

> The key is not to prioritize what's on your schedule, but to schedule your priorities.
>
> Stephen Covey

The two-step time management rule is:

1. Plan your day to achieve your goals.
2. Stick to your plan.

When you develop the habit of starting on your most important task before doing anything else, your success is ensured. Following are twelve ways to get more things done in less time. In sales, time mastery is life mastery.

1. **Set goals**. Write down your goals and objectives before you begin. Decide exactly what you want. Clarity is essential. *Goal setting and time planning go hand in hand.* You cannot effectively plan your time without setting goals. Also, you cannot achieve your goals without effectively planning

your time. Knowing what you must do each day to achieve your annual sales target helps you spend your time on what will matter most. At the beginning of your workday, start immediately on your most important task, and then work without stopping until the job is 100 per cent complete. This is the real key to high performance and maximum personal productivity. I personally prefer to spend the first half-hour of each day in making a daily agenda report. At the end of this chapter, you will find a daily agenda report for easy reference. It consists of two parts. (1) What did I get done yesterday? and (2) What is my plan for today?

2. **Geographically plan your calls well.** Reduce your travelling time, and increase face time with customers. Divide your sales territory into quadrants. Resolve to work in one quadrant each day or each half-day. Cluster all your calls in that quadrant for that time period.
3. **Plan for your appointments.** Some salespeople try to meet customers without an appointment, and as result waste a lot of time waiting and travelling. While driving, some salespeople, in place of listening to audiobooks related to sales skills, prefer to listen to the radio, which is of no use in achieving their sales goal. Sometimes salespeople lose half a day because they did not reconfirm an appointment. Sometimes, upon reaching the meeting venue, salespeople find that the key person has already left or is busy in another meeting and unable to meet that day.
4. **Apply the 80–20 rule to everything.** Twenty per cent of your activities will account for eighty per cent of your results. Always concentrate your efforts on that twenty per cent.
5. **Prioritize.** Before you begin work on a list of tasks, take a few moments to organize them by value and priority so you

can be sure of working on your most important activities first. Identify the three things you do in your work that account for 90 per cent of your contribution, and focus on getting those things done before anything else. You will then have more time for your family and personal life. In sales, the three most important activities are *prospecting*, *presenting*, and *closing*. Focus on key result areas. *Do the most important thing first.*

6. **Prepare thoroughly before you begin.** Have everything you need at hand before you start. Assemble your papers/ sales quotes, business cards, tools, product brochures, pens, notes diary, etc. The best salespeople memorize their product specifications. Alternatively, as smartphones are very popular, you can save all of your brochures, technical specification sheets, and presentations in an app such as Dropbox. I use Dropbox. It's very helpful.
7. **Upgrade your key skills.** The more knowledgeable and skilled you are when it comes to your key tasks, the faster you can start them and the sooner you can get them done. As a successful salesperson you must learn to:

    - Identify customer needs clearly.
    - Present properly.
    - Answer objections intelligently.
    - Close the sale professionally.

8. **Put the pressure on yourself.** Imagine that you have to travel out of the country for annual leave and you will be gone for a month. Work as if you had to get all your major tasks completed before your date of departure. Develop a sense of urgency. Make a habit of moving fast on your key tasks.

9. **Maximize your personal power.** Identify your periods of highest mental and physical energy each day, and schedule your most important and demanding tasks for these times. Get lots of rest so you can perform at your best. Personally I prefer to finish my most difficult and most important jobs between 8 a.m. and 10 a.m.
10. **Motivate yourself into action.** No one will motivate you; you must motivate yourself. Look for the good in every situation. Focus on the solution rather than on the problem. Always be optimistic and constructive. Your main goals are to:
    a. generate more enquiries and
    b. increase your strike rate by converting enquiries into confirmed orders.
11. **Get out of the technological time sinks.** Use technology to improve the quality of your communications, but do not allow yourself to become a slave to it. Avoid checking for messages and emails frequently. I personally prefer to check emails once in the morning and once in the evening. Sometimes I check after lunch too.
12. **Practise these proven time management techniques every day until they become your habit.**

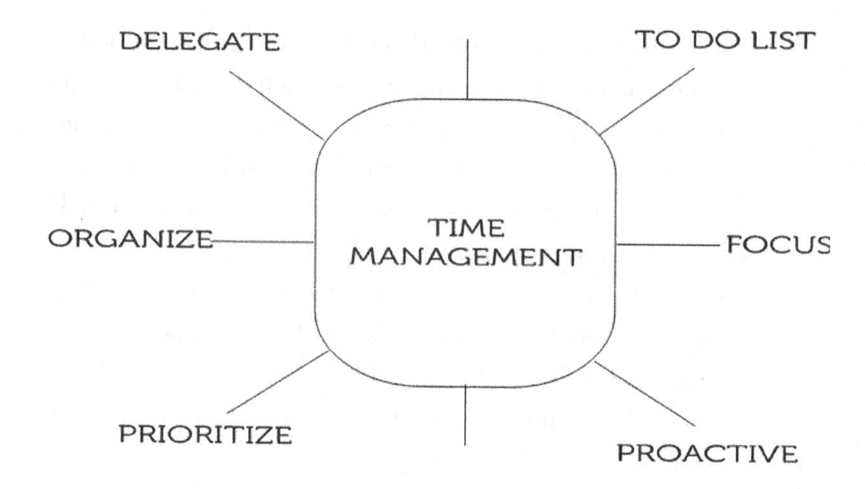

Optimize Your Time at the Office by Developing Six Work Habits

Apply the following six habits to your workday and you will find very positive improvements in your overall performance. With these habits, you can use your time more effectively than before. Note any particular work habit you have which is helping you to use your time more effectively and improving your contribution to your company.

1. For your first few minutes in the office, recall what you got done the day before and what your plan is for today. Lack of evaluation of daily performance is one of common reasons why salespeople fail. It is a good idea to jot down on a two-column piece of paper or to type into an Excel spreadsheet the things you got accomplished the day before and the things in front of you today. With regard to what you got done the day before, ask, *Have I achieved my daily goals in light of my sales target?* With regard to your plan for today, ask, *Is it in line with my daily goals?*

2. For the next few minutes, ponder or analyse what you got done the day before. Ask the following two questions of yourself:
   - What are the three main activities which I did well yesterday and which were of the highest value in light of my contribution to my company?
   - What are the activities which only I can do and make a real difference with? How I can make these better?
3. Clear your desk of all papers except those related to the immediate problem at hand.
4. Do things in the order of their importance. You should do the most difficult job first. Resist the temptation to do the easy and unimportant things first.
5. When you face a problem, solve it right then and there if you have the facts necessary to make a decision. Don't put off decisions.
6. Learn to organize, delegate, and supervise. Focus on those important jobs which cannot be delegated and which require your involvement.

Manage Your Time

Or It Will Manage You

You manage what you measure. I personally prefer to make only two reports. These are:

- **Daily agenda report**

  For the first thirty minutes of every workday, I prefer to finish this report, which consists of two paragraphs: what I got done yesterday and what my plan is for today.

- **Monthly sales report**
- Every Monday at 9 a.m., my sales team has a sales meeting in which we discuss the enquiries we generated in the last week, the orders we closed, the reasons for any orders we lost, customers we visited, and so forth.

Daily Agenda Report

	DAILY AGENDA REPORT		
SALES	EXECUTIVE NAME	Date	
	What I have done yesterday?		
1			
2			
3			
4			
5			
6			
	What is my plan for today?		
1			
2			
3			
4			
5			
6			
	Support required from the management		
1			
2			
	Remarks by Sales Manager		
1			
2			
	Notes by Sales Professional		
1			
2			

Monthly Sales Report

Monthly Sales Report	
Remarks	Order Confirmed
	Live and follow up
	Quoted but no feedback / budgetory purpose only
	Order Lost

Major Orders Won

S/N	Date	Customer	Product details	Qty.	Currency	Order Value	Remarks
1							Order Confirmed.
2							
3							
4							
5							
		TOTAL					

Quotation Status

S/N	Date	Customer	Product details	Qty.	Cur	Order Value	Remarks
1							
2							
3							
4							
5							
6							
7							
8							
9							
10							
		TOTAL					

Projection for next three (3) months

S/N		Customer	Product details	Qty.	Currency	Order Value	Confidence (100% / 70% / 50%)
1							
2							
3							
4							
		TOTAL					

Support needed from the management

1	
2	

CHAPTER 19

What Makes Salespeople Fail

I have noticed over my several-year sales career that salespeople fail for the following reasons:

- They do not learn sales skills.
  Lack of sales training is the major reason why salespeople fail.
- They spend more time in the office and less time with customers.
  In the selling profession, business doesn't come to us; we have to go out and get it. Salespeople need to perform some office tasks like checking and to responding email, calling customers, coordinating with the logistics department for timely delivery of goods to customers, attending sales meetings, completing monthly sales reports and daily agenda reports, and maintaining a customer contact list, so they need to learn good work habits to minimize time spent in the office. This was discussed in Chapter 18 – Time Management.
- They do not follow up in a timely manner.
  One of the reasons salespeople fail is because they do not follow up with customers in a timely manner. *Too much or too little follow-up is dangerous.* Timely follow-up builds credibility and trust with potential customers. *Good follow-up keeps the customer informed, and informed customers see you as more*

reliable than other salespeople. Following up shows your caring attitude and makes the customer feel important and happy. If you don't want to lose sales to your competition, then focus on providing timely follow-up. Customers don't prefer to work with those salespeople whom they find unreliable. You should use the right combination of direct emails, telephonic calls, and in-person visits to make your follow-ups more effective, as discussed in Chapter 1 – Selling.

Other major reasons that people fail in the sales profession are as follows:

- absence of a positive mental attitude (discussed in Chapter 2)
- lack of self-discipline (discussed in Chapter 3)
- lack of ambition and a burning desire (discussed in Chapter 4)
- an unpleasant personality (discussed in Chapter 5)
- lack of team spirit (discussed in Chapter 5)
- untrustworthiness (discussed in Chapter 5)
- lack of synergy between the sales department and the marketing department (discussed in Chapter 5)
- lack of clarity about roles and goals (discussed in Chapter 6)
- lack of hard work and persistence (discussed in Chapter 7)
- poor communication skills when talking with customers (discussed in Chapter 8)
- inability to deal with customers (discussed in Chapter 9)
- failure to practice the sales presentation (discussed in Chapter 10)
- lack of knowledge about the product being sold (discussed in Chapter 10)
- unwillingness to learn new sales skills (discussed in Chapter 10)
- fear of rejection (discussed in Chapter 11)

- fear of failure (discussed in Chapter 11)
- lack of enthusiasm (discussed in Chapter 11)
- lack of sales skills (discussed in Chapters 12, 13, and 14)
- lack of knowledge about the market and the competition (discussed in Chapter 15)
- targeting the wrong segment of customers (discussed in Chapter 15)
- lack of understanding of product positioning (discussed in Chapter 16)
- inability to develop positive rapport with customers (discussed in Chapter 17)
- inability to manage time well (discussed in Chapter 18)
- failure to spending sufficient time in prospecting, presenting, and closing (discussed in Chapter 18).

Many times, salespeople fail because the sales targets have been made unilaterally and without any consideration of resources. A good sales professional should get involved and ask the company to jointly identify the goals and provide the necessary resources to achieve the desired results (as discussed in Chapter 6).

Other times, salespeople fail because they fail to plan for their appointments with customers. They try to meet customers without having an appointment and as a result waste a lot of time waiting and travelling (as discussed in Chapter 8).

Some salespeople neglect to practise their sales presentation. This, combined with a lack of knowledge about their product, the market, and their competition, makes it difficult for them to get the order from customers (as discussed in Chapter 10).

Some salespeople are unable to get along with their colleagues and their boss. They just lack team spirit. They forget that "together everyone achieves more." They lack a positive mental attitude and have an unpleasant personality (as discussed in Chapter 2 and Chapter 5).

Some unsuccessful salespeople fail to evaluate their daily performance. There is famous saying: "If you continue to do the same thing, then you will continue to get the same result." Continuous improvement is the minimum requirement for success in a sales career, as sales is both a very challenging and a very rewarding occupation (as discussed in Chapter 18).

Finally, some salespeople are unable to handle angry customers. They yell back when the customer shouts at them. They don't realize that the customer is angry not with them but about the product or service. This attitude makes an angry customer more angry. Not only do salespeople like this lose repeat business, but also they look bad in the eyes of management when the angry customer takes his or her complaint to the next level (as discussed in Chapter 9).

CHAPTER 20

Ethics in Selling

> A salesperson's ethics and values contribute more to sales success than do techniques or strategies.
>
> Ron Willingham

> Some people know the price of everything but value of nothing.
>
> Oscar Wilde

Professional salespeople follow a strict code of ethics. Practising ethics in selling is a must for long-term business relationships with customers. You will get repeat business from your customers if your current dealings are based on honesty and trust. Customers give their business to whom they know, like, and trust. The good sales professional sells products or services, but never sells against their conscience. Ethical salespeople make their conscience and values their guiding principles. Every behaviour and transaction is guided by those principles, and this way of acting becomes the good salesperson's philosophy. This philosophy works as a lighthouse, guiding the salesperson in the right direction. The good salesperson lives by the principles of ethical selling. Ethical behaviour is not a strategy but a way of life. A good sales professional does not have different ethical standards for different situations. His morality doesn't change from person to person or from situation to situation.

There is a story involving Abraham Lincoln that is worth sharing. A very successful lawyer who became a politician and was elected US president in 1861, Lincoln came from a poor family. One time a man brought a case to him to consider. After Lincoln looked over the facts, he said, "Technically this case is OK, but ethically it is not OK. I will not take your case."

The man said, "I am willing to pay your fee."

Lincoln said, "My fee is not the issue. The issue is that when it comes time for me to argue your case in front of a judge, I will keep saying to myself in the back of my mind, *Lincoln, you are a liar. Lincoln, you are a liar.* I could not live with myself."

Some people make money at the cost of selling their souls. Oscar Wilde said, "Some people know the price of everything, but value of nothing.

Learn when to walk away from business.

Relationships are built on win-win principles and not win-lose propositions. In the following situations, it is better to walk away from business:

- when you are asked to compromise your values
- when you are asked to cheat your company
- when the prospect is asking for a price which is below your cost.

Following are some examples of unethical temptations for a salesperson:

- to conceal some important information about a product or service from a customer in order to get their business;
- to make false claims about the product or service in order to achieve a sales target;
- to offer a customer an expensive "gift" in return for their business;
- to put non-business-related expenses on your expense account;
- to share confidential information about one customer with another in order to close a sale;
- to go out for company business but do personal work instead;
- to give false sales and visit reports to management;
- to misuse the company's assets in any way.

Common excuses for unethical behaviour:

- It's for the benefit of the company, as it will increase the chance of closing the sale.
- Competitors are doing it. If we don't do it, we will lose out to the competition.
- It's necessary. Nobody will know. It's not going to hurt anyone.

Guidelines for making ethical decisions:

- Respect the law of the land. Make sure your selling decisions are legal.
- Sell in such a way that is consistent with your company beliefs/values.

- Sell in such a way that is based on values and not on personal gain.

Recommendations for salespeople who give gifts to prospects and/or customers:

- Give a gift only after the sale is made, preferably on a special occasion. Personally, I prefer to give my customers a gift on the occasion of New Year or at the annual parties of my regular customers. Ensure that the gift is simple and thoughtful, so it can't be interpreted as a bribe.
- Before giving a gift, make sure it is within your customer's company policy to receive gifts from salespeople.

> Integrity
>
> is choosing your thoughts and actions based on values rather than personal gains

ABOUT THE AUTHOR

After receiving his Bachelor in Technology (BTech) degree in mechanical engineering in year 2000 from one of the premier universities of India, Aligarh Muslim University, Zeaur Rahman started his career as a mechanical engineer. After three years at that job – one year in India and two years in Saudi Arabia – he switched to the field of sales, which he found to be very interesting, as every day he had the chance to meet new people and work amid tough competition, rising to the challenge of getting customers' business. After working six years in Saudi Arabia, Zeaur moved to the United Arab Emirates to explore better growth opportunities. In the year 2008, the world faced a great recession. All of a sudden, projects stopped and companies were closed. Because of the sudden reduction in business, almost every company downsized. Lots of people lost their jobs. At that point, Zeaur realized that he needed to get serious about honing his sales ability if he wanted to retain his sales job. He started listening to audiobooks and podcasts related to sales during travelling, and reading sales- and motivation-related books at weekends. He is very grateful to the many writers from whom he has learnt a lot.

Zeaur Rahman enrolled himself into a two-year evening MBA programme at S. P. Jain Centre of Management, Dubai, in 2009. He is very thankful to all his teachers at S. P. Jain Centre of Management, as after receiving his MBA he found himself a more confident and better sales professional.

People learn in one of two ways: either by reading or by associating with smarter people. Since the year 2000, Zeaur has been working. During all those years on the job, he associated with many smart, educated, and experienced professionals and learnt a lot from all of them. Zeaur is grateful to all the companies where he has worked, especially German–Gulf Enterprises, his current employer.

As Zeaur has benefitted immensely from others' knowledge, it is his humble pleasure to share his experiences and what he has learnt in his many years as a sales professional. You can reach him by email at zeaur2000@gmail.com. His LinkedIn profile is found at linkedin.com/in/zeaur.

Printed in the United States
By Bookmasters